C0-AKH-444

ABRAHAM ELLIS

· · · · ·

THE

SOCIAL SECURITY

FRAUD

· · · · ·

The Foundation for Economic Education, Inc.
Irvington-on-Hudson, New York

To NAN

• • • •

The Social Security Fraud

Copyright © 1996 by the Foundation for Economic Education

All rights reserved. No part of this book may be reproduced or transmitted in any form or by any means, electronic or mechanical, including photocopying, recording or by any information storage and retrieval systems without permission in writing from the publisher, except by a reviewer, who may quote brief passages in a review.

The Foundation for Economic Education, Inc.
30 South Broadway
Irvington-on-Hudson, NY 10533
(914) 591–7230

Publisher's Cataloging in Publication
(Prepared by Quality Books, Inc.)

Ellis, Abraham, 1911–
    The Social Security fraud / Abraham Ellis.
    p. cm.
    Includes index
    ISBN 1-57246-053-9
    1. Social security—United States. I. Title.
    HD7125.E55   1996

                               368.4'3'00973
                               QBI96–20180

Library of Congress Catalog Card Number: 96-84490

Second edition, May 1996
Cover design by Beth R. Bowlby
Manufactured in the United States of America

Introduction

• • • •

History teaches that we must be on our guard to protect liberty when the government's intention is beneficial. The U.S. Congress unfortunately did not heed this lesson when it passed President Franklin D. Roosevelt's proposals for a Social Security system. Since then the scheme not only has grown into a mammoth transfer apparatus but also has become the central pillar supporting our social and political structure. It is the most popular and formidable of all entitlement programs. Well nigh untouchable, it is exempt from political review and budget restraint even when massive deficits are suffered and lesser programs are cut. The Reagan Administration confirmed it and the Johnson Medicare system when it not only kept both off the "cutting table" but also reinforced them with "catastrophic insurance" and "nursing care." The Republican "Contract with America" even promised to *improve* the benefits by allowing senior citizens "to earn more without losing Social Security benefits" and to reduce the taxes they have to pay on those benefits.

The system is powerful and influential because it has the enthusiastic support of an important, growing social class: the elderly. Some thirty-five million elderly Americans sing the praises and beat the drum for Social Security and Medicare which has made them beneficiaries of the most massive transfer system ever devised. They glorify it because they are reaping a hundredfold gain on the money they contributed. The maximum contribution from the beginning through 1949 amounted to one percent on $3,000 annual income, or $30 a year. In 1950 it rose to 1.5 percent, or $45, and thereafter continued to creep

3

up in small increments. Few old-timers, if any, contributed more than $1,000 with interest on interest during their working years. By drawing Social Security now and availing themselves of Medicare benefits many retirees enjoy returns which are hundredfold or, after a few Medicare weeks in a hospital, even thousandfold. They cry out in fear against any suggestion of Social Security reform.

They need not panic! We see no real opposition on the political and intellectual horizon. Few writers dare to touch the system; legislators without exception would enlarge it and increase its outlays by many billions of dollars. A solitary critical argument points at its income statement and balance sheet. "The system will run out of funds," we are told. "It will be bankrupt in the year 2020 or 2030. We can no longer afford it." Such arguments actually are counterproductive as they invite a search for additional funds. They do not touch the core of the system, but implicitly accept and approve of it by limiting the discussion to its finances. The "empty-pocket argument" evades the discussion of the immorality of the system; its intrinsic exploitation of one class by another, fostering economic and social conflict; its discouragement of saving and self-reliance; its erosion of the moral fiber of the people making them believe that the paternal state rather than their own efforts is responsible for their well-being. In short, the Social Security system provides a fertile breeding ground for a political and economic command system. The forerunner and model of all modern Social Security systems, the German system of the 1880s, paved the way; it conditioned the German mind and psyche for the omnipresent, omnipotent state and caused the downfall of Germany in two World Wars.

The American system of Social Security is comparable in design and appearance. It has fundamental structural flaws which have given rise to a great number of reform proposals.

Some would write the old prescription: more benefits for more retirees and higher tax extractions from the working population. Some proposals would make a few minor cosmetic adjustments such as increasing the retirement age by several years, while some would freeze the cost-of-living adjustments. Some would even reorganize the system along the lines of a private retirement savings structure.

Several legislators would reduce Social Security payroll taxes by 1 percent each for both employers and employees and place the savings into mandatory Individual Social Security Retirement Accounts. Individuals would own the accounts and instruct bonded money managers on how to invest the funds. Upon retirement the benefits would consist of two parts: the regular Social Security payments and the annuity income from the investment account.

Another bill would raise the full-benefit retirement age to 70, phased in over 30 years, limit some COLAs (Cost of Living Allowance), reduce spousal benefits, cut Social Security payroll taxes by 1.5 percent, and require contributions to IRAs for all members under age 55, starting January 1, 2000. Another yet would reduce the benefits by CPI (Consumer Price Index) calculation adjustments to prevent benefit increases beyond actual inflation. It, too, would allow workers to reduce their OASDI (Old-Age and Survivors Insurance and Disability) taxes by 1.5 percent which would have to be deposited in their personal retirement accounts.

Several senators introduced legislation that would delay the full-benefit age to 70 by 2030, limit COLAs, reduce spousal benefits, and allow workers to invest 2 percent of their OASDI payroll taxes in their own personal investment plan. The proposal also would allow the Social Security Administration to invest up to 25 percent of its total funds, presently amounting to some $400 billion, in stocks and bonds, which would make the Administration the biggest player in the capital market.

Many Social Security reformers like to point to Chile and draw conclusions from its reorganization and privatization experience since 1981. José Piñera who as Secretary of Labor led the reorganization readily admits that it was no complete privatization (Cato Policy Report, July/August 1995); the government is still responsible for many features of the new system. It requires that at least one half of portfolio assets be held in government securities. It forces workers to contribute no less than 10 percent and no more than 20 percent of their wages into an account they own outright. At the inauguration of the reform the workers were given the option of staying in the old system or joining the new. Those who joined the new were given "recognition bonds" which compensated them for their contributions to the old system. Young workers entering the labor market have no such choice, they are all assigned to the new.

Today, some 15 years later, the system is paying old-age pensions that are 40 to 50 percent higher than those paid by the old system. The Chilean savings rate has soared to that of the Asian tigers. Moreover, the popularity of the system has permitted the government to proceed with yet other privatizations such as the energy and telecommunication industries.

Few American reformers look toward Chile for inspiration and guidance. The Chilean reform, after all, was introduced and enforced by a military junta that had seized power in September 1973. This political background together with the political repression which continued throughout the 1980s make any reform à la Chile unsavory and unacceptable. Moreover, any reform introduced by brute force tends to be short-lived even if it is accompanied by lengthy explanation and indoctrination. This is why we believe that the last chapter of the Chilean reform has not yet been written.

In a free society all power flows from public opinion, which is the opinion of a few thousand thought leaders. Government is founded on public opinion as are public laws and regulations. Economic and social reforms are guided by public opinion which, in our age of electronic media, may change swiftly and unexpectedly. It usually is unmoved by cost and economy. It chooses between good and bad or, what it believes to be, moral and evil. Things are called good or bad in reference to the public perception of morality. This is why any reform of the Social Security system must proceed from the high ground of goodness and morality; any other ground, no matter how rational and economical, is bound to disappoint.

Abraham Ellis' *The Social Security Fraud* seizes the high ground of morality which permits him to attack courageously with conviction and force. To him, the system is an offshoot of "the something-for-nothing philosophy, the free lunch syndrome." It permeates American politics and leads politicians to pander to the numerically powerful group of elderly voters. In addition, there are the jobholders and their families who administer the vast Social Security program. What politician has the courage to tell the truth? Yet, Abe Ellis does not despair; he closes on a positive note that points toward the light of freedom:

"Security will never come from a Social Security system in an expansive Welfare State. It can only be realized when the source of security is discovered to lie within the individual himself. This simple truth makes it mandatory that the collectivist trend acquiring such great momentum in the 20th century must be reversed. It may be too late because power is not freely abdicated. The remedy requires that the people must reacquire the liberties they gradually surrendered to the State." They must regain liberty with wisdom and virtue which are their own reward.

Hans F. Sennholz

Contents

• • • •

I

• • • • • • • • •

The Birth of Social Security

AFTER the 1929 stock market crash, America suffered a massive stroke and was paralyzed. In the 1930s banks were closing their doors, many never to reopen, factories were shutting down and farmers were in revolt preventing local sheriffs at the point of a shot-gun, from executing court decrees directing them to foreclose on defaulted mortgages. In the winter of 1935, 6 years after the onset of the depression, 22 million Americans or almost 20 percent of the entire population were on the dole. Not all of them were selling apples on city streets to supplement their relief payments. The grim joke was current that hotel clerks in major cities were inquiring whether prospective guests wished to rent rooms on upper floors for sleeping or jumping.

America was just as rich in natural resources in the thirties as it had been a decade before. Its factories and farms were, if anything, more modern, its people just as industrious; it had had a long period of peace and had met with no catastrophic disasters. What then went wrong? When President Franklin D. Roosevelt delivered his inaugural address on that gloomy

Saturday, March 4, 1933, he succinctly voiced the prevailing mood when he said "Only foolish optimism can deny the dark realities of the moment". Financier Bernard Baruch had just said three weeks before, "I regard the condition of the country the most serious in its history".

It was natural that with the worsening of the depression and from 1930 to 1935, the Federal Government invented and organized crash programs on a temporary relief basis hoping that as in all prior economic depressions, the private sector would ultimately recover and absorb the unemployed. After all, the business cycle was nothing new.

Among the many such programs adopted by the Federal Government in its attempt to hasten the recovery of the economy which seemed obstinately determined to remain sick, were the NRA, WPA, PWA, AAA, CCC, CWA, FERA, RFC, etc. (I use initials for the sake of brevity as the names if spelled out in full would be of little meaning anyway to the post-depression generations of today.) Peculiarly, they seemed to be of no help whatsoever in alleviating the crisis which continued to deepen.

It took the massive rearmament occasioned by Hitler's rise and the approach of the Second World War to artificially stimulate the economy and quickly solve the unemployment problem in both America and Germany. Nine years after the start of the depression things were just as bad. Hitler, however, succeeded in ending the depression where the college professors, the politicians, and the New Deal had failed.

It was this depressing and horrible state of affairs in America, that gave birth to the Social Security System as we know it now. It is inconceivable that Social Security legislation could have been passed in the halcyon days of 1928. It needed the right climate.

Plans and suggestions for ending the depression were coming from all sides. Even the medical profession was prominently represented. In 1933, Dr. Francis E. Townsend came out for a flat pension of $200. per month to everyone who attained the magical age of 60. One of the conditions of his plan which gained great popularity, was that the recipients had to spend the $200. each month as they received it. The Townsend plan was to be financed by a 2 percent transactions tax. Radio programs mushroomed plugging the good Doctor's version of security for the aged and Townsend Clubs were being organized by the thousands. In addition, substantial support was developing in Congress itself for this simplistic, crack-pot scheme.

Obviously the prevailing mood called for action—which was not long in coming. In 1934, a study group was organized under the auspices of the Federal Government, which submitted its report to Congress early in 1935. Everybody was for it. It received enthusiastic bipartisan support, even to the extent of the Republicans' denouncing President Roosevelt for having waited so long in getting a Social Security program before Congress. It became the law of the land on August 14, 1935.

This child of the depression was named the "Social Security Act of 1935." It provided for Federal grants-in-aid to approved state programs for aid to the aged and established a national system of old age insurance. In addition, with respect to unemployment insurance, a system of federal-state cooperation was adopted in lieu of leaving unemployment compensation exclusively to the individual states. As to the unemployment insurance program, without going into too great detail, the Social Security Act of 1935 provided for a tax-offset scheme intended to stimulate action by the states in accordance with minimum standards rather than to define what each state had to do. In such cases the federal government allocated certain funds to all the states which conformed to its requirements. Within two years all the states qualified, meeting these minimum standards, but still leaving themselves plenty of leeway to choose the type of unemployment compensation plan they wanted which varied as to coverage, contributions, reserves, and benefits.

From these grants-in-aid the qualifying states were enabled to make cash payments to the needy aged, dependent children, the blind, and those permanently and wholly disabled, supplementing federal funds with their own. There were additional appropriations in the form of welfare services for mothers and children in rural areas and in economically distressed places, and for crippled, homeless, dependent children. Also those children who were found to be in danger of becoming delinquent were provided for.

Health insurance was also seriously considered for inclusion in the original Social Security Act, since this type of social insurance was prominent in Europe. England had had a health insurance law since 1911. However, it was not until some thirty years after the passage of the Social Security Act that medical coverage in America became a part of the Social Security system.

It is not within the scope of this work to examine in detail the unemployment insurance or the public assistance to the needy features or the medicare provisions of the Social Security system, except incidentally. What is examined is the general search for security that in recent years has tended to incline heavily towards the Federal Government. Through the Social Security System it has willingly assumed the role of providing this security, resulting in a great proliferation of new activities in an attempt to insure against the hazards of old age and illness.

The primary concerns of this book are with the main features of the Social Security System which provide cash income for superannuated, retired, and pensioned workers and provide for payments to their wives, widows, dependent children and their aged parents, and with the methods of administering and financing such payments. In short, Government old-age pensions will come in for most of the criticism and evaluation, as that is the avowed primary object of the bounty of the Social Security System and is by far its most important and costly ingredient.

In particular, an analysis will be made both as to the promise and performance of the Social Security Act in attempting to satisfy the aspirations of the vast majority of Americans for the good life. The pitfalls and dangers along the road will also be examined with a view to learning whether or not they are inherent in the process, and also whether the original concept of a limited Government contemplated in the Constitution should be radically altered to conform to its new role, designed to erect a protective barrier and provide a shield for its citizens against the insecurity of modern life.

In the following pages I propose to establish that a great fraud is being perpetrated upon the American people. It may be by deliberate design or perhaps as a result of ignorance but in either event it constitutes fraud and deceit.

It is the purpose of this book to examine the Social Security System in depth and to let the chips fall where they may. It is contemplated that it will disturb many and throw doubt on the validity and soundness of the entire Social Security program and its administration, with the faint but fervent hope that remedial legislation will follow.

It is entirely possible, as a side effect, that some readers might even appreciate the advantage of a dose of insecurity as an alternative to that government-administered security from the cradle to the grave, which seems to be the obsession of our times.

It should be noted, incidentally, that the devout hope that Social Security would eliminate or at least significantly decrease the need for large scale public assistance has proved illusory. On the front page of the New York Times of November 1, 1968, for example, it was reported that public welfare payments had supplanted education costs as New York City's biggest expense item. While Social Security benefits were at an all time high, welfare rolls, too, were rising at the rate of more than 20,000 recipients a month. The relief rolls continue to expand throughout the country and there is more social unrest and less security, despite the constantly increasing of Social Security benefits and the waging of ever bigger and better "wars on poverty."

In a period of generally great prosperity throughout America, and after more than three decades of constant modifications and tinkering with the Social Security System, it is quite apparent that it has not provided true economic security and the fundamental causes of insecurity are very much still with us. Thirty-five years after the passage of the Social Security Act we find the average monthly government check mailed to retired workers is $105.80. The promise that his Social Security pension would thus dignify the retired worker by giving him that which he himself earned so that he would not have to apply for public welfare in his old age has proved illusory. The Social Security System has clearly not proven to be a panacea for the dilemma of poverty in the midst of plenty nor has it alleviated the fears of economic insecurity.

Even if nothing concrete or practical is accomplished by this examination of that problem and the reasons for the failure in this field of government intervention on such a huge scale with a Social Security administration expense alone of close to a billion dollars a year, at least if some readers are alerted to the dangers which the Social Security System contains and thus become aware of the tendencies inherent in its constant expansion, this work will not have been in vain.

II

• • • • • • • • •

Some Historical Background

"THIRTY years ago it was different, thirty years ago we had that empty feeling. Because of Social Security you're not afraid of tomorrow."

"I got mine three years ago. I kissed it and said, God Bless America."

These were typical of the comments of some three thousand elderly Americans, reported in the *New York Times* of August 16, 1965, who made a pilgrimage to President Franklin D. Roosevelt's home in Hyde Park to commemorate his signing of the Social Security Act thirty years before.

Ida Fuller was a law secretary in Vermont in 1935 when the first Social Security Act was passed. Her employers started deducting one percent from her pay check in 1937 when she was sixty-three years old. She retired two years later. Her first check came on February 1, 1940, in the amount of $22.54 and she has already received over 370 checks. She had paid less than $70.00 into the Social Security System when she retired. Miss Fuller had the distinction of being the first person to receive a Social Security check.

Within four months after her retirement she received more from Social Security than she had contributed. Her $70.00 contribution has already paid her back over $12,000 and as this is written she is in her 96th year and still collecting at the rate of $90 per month. Undoubtedly a fabulous investment for Ida and she is duly grateful.

This cornucopia was by no means limited to the early retirees like Ida Fuller. People who retired in 1942, as a class, will get back in Social Security checks approximately 60 times as much as they paid in Social Security taxes. If a worker, 50 years of age, had paid the maximum tax like Ida from 1937 on, and had retired not two years later as she did, but fifteen years later, he would have had $489.00 deducted from his salary. A like amount would have been taxed to his employer, making a total of $978.00. As the law then stood, he and his wife would start collecting $102.80 a month, so that in ten months he would recoup more than he and his employer had paid in fifteen years. According to his life expectancy, which at sixty-five would be thirteen years, he could expect to get twelve years of "free social security." Certainly a sweet deal for him too, and he and all those in the same fortunate class are undoubtedly great advocates of Social Security and not particularly concerned about where the money is coming from either.

Now there is another side of the coin. Not everyone is so fortunate as Ida Fuller. Take, for example, the case of the well-known and widely syndicated financial writer Sylvia Porter. She lamented in an article in the *New York Post* of December 10, 1968, that within a few weeks she would start paying a new high annual maximum of $374.40 in Social Security taxes. Her boss, of course, would pay a like amount, making a total 1969 Social Security tax bill of $748.80. She complained that for this plus all the previous amounts she paid into the Social Security System during her working years, her Social Security benefits when she reaches the retirement age of 65 will be exactly zero. The reason for this deplorable state of the affairs of Sylvia as contrasted with Ida is obvious. Ida retired but Sylvia plans to go on working at 65, confidently expects to earn a good deal more than $1680 per year and will thus be disqualified from collecting her Social Security. To make things worse, contrary to the provision in the 1935 law which exempted from Social Security tax the income of workers over 65, Sylvia's earnings will now continue to be taxed after her 65th birthday for Social Security benefits she may never get. There are many people, writers included, who still enjoy working all their lives.

In the original Social Security law, it was also provided that a worker or his estate was sure to get back at least what was paid into his account. If he died before collecting his Social Security benefits, a formula was set up to reimburse his family or he could dispose of his cash benefit in his last will and testament to whomever he desired. The Government did not get a windfall as it does now in millions of cases since the 1939 Amendment was passed which cancelled the money-back guarantee.

When the Social Security Act became law, almost half the working population were not included. However, as time went on, all the escape hatches were closed and even the large numbers of affluent professionals and other self-employed have been forced into the System.

I don't think Ida Fuller wanted Sylvia Porter to contribute to her support for thirty years nor do I imagine that Sylvia Porter would voluntarily have done so. Nevertheless that is exactly how it worked out indirectly with neither one being consulted and Ida's gain is Sylvia's loss.

The story of Ida and Sylvia is an incongruous result of the

search for economic security which has been man's concern from the beginning of time. On June 8, 1934, President Franklin D. Roosevelt in his message to Congress said:

> Among our objectives I place the security of men, women, and children of the Nation, first. —Fear and worry, based on unknown danger, contribute to social unrest and economic demoralization. If, as our Constitution tells us, our Federal Government was established among other things 'to promote the general welfare,' it is our plain duty to provide for that security upon which welfare depends. Next winter we may well undertake the great task of furthering the security of the citizen and his family through social insurance.

After the speech, as we have seen, Roosevelt appointed a Committee on Economic Security to report and make recommendations. It rendered its report on January 15, 1935, urging the establishment of a Social Security program, stating:

> A program of economic security, as we vision it, must have as its primary aim the assurance of an adequate income to each human being in childhood, youth, middle age, or old age —in sickness or in health. It must provide safeguards against all of the hazards leading to destitution and dependency.

On August 14, 1935, when Franklin D. Roosevelt signed the Social Security Act passed by Congress, security for the individual thus for the first time became a matter of Federal government concern in America.

At the time of passage of the Social Security Act more people were getting relief than were paying an income tax. Social Security numbers were considered to be of such vital importance, that when the Social Security Act was enacted into law and the cards were first issued, many card holders went as far as to tatoo their numbers on their skin so as to insure against loss. The passing years have not diminished their importance although until his retirement from the working force, the average worker is only aware of the existence of the Social Security System because of the amount taken out of his pay envelope before he can lay his hands on it.

Prior to the great depression which started in 1929, relief for the poor was considered to be basically a local responsibility, the concern of private philanthropy and religious organizations, as well as the community in which those in need lived. Until a short time before that depression, the Elizabethan system of local relief for the poor prevailed in America along the same general lines as in England. As a matter of fact even before the Elizabethan Poor Law of 1601 in England it was considered a community responsibility as well as a religious obligation to take care of the sick and the poor —those who were unable to care for themselves with no relatives to assume that burden. It was not until 1863 in America that Massachusetts became the first state to be concerned with the poor at the state level and by 1913, 27 states through State Boards of Charities supervised local poorhouses, and two states, Montana and Nevada by 1925 had their own old-age pension statutes on the books.

As late as 1931, concern for the poor was still considered to be basically a matter of local responsibility. Not one dollar was ever contributed by the national government for the relief of the unemployed, or as a matter of fact for any other form of relief for the poor and the aged.

With the passage of the Social Security Act in 1935, for the first time the national government acknowledged a permanent responsibility in this area. When the Social Security legislation was first introduced, the only state that had even an unemployment insurance law was Wisconsin.

The reverence for the Social Security System exemplified by this pilgrimage to the shrine at Hyde Park referred to in the opening paragraph of this chapter grows stronger with the passing years. The benefits are constantly enlarged so as to include broad compulsory health insurance, as well as to make the old-age and survivors insurance system a retirement system with greater and greater benefits. The number of beneficiaries is constantly growing and the thought of life without Social Security has become inconceivable. Today more than 25 million men, women and children are receiving cash benefits monthly from their central government. It has become an integral part of the American way of life.

The dictionary defines security as the state or feeling of being free from fear, care, want, danger, etc. These seem to be worth-while aims and what follows will be an examination of the policies of the government of the United States, and incidentally those of other countries, in setting up and administering a national Social Security System in order to free its people from economic "fear, care and want."

By adopting a national Social Security program, the Federal Government implicitly assumes that its workers cannot or will not adequately provide for their own security and that it is the function of the state, therefore, to provide for them in their time of need. After all, the essence of a paternalistic welfare state is that some portion of the money people earn is taken from them, and then spent or disposed of by the takers in ways other than the wage-earner would have chosen if he were permitted to retain his hard earned money. Presumably these other ways are wiser and better for him. If this were not so, compulsory Social Security would make no sense at all, and the justification for its existence would disappear.

The security of the individual in his economic life has now

become the province of the federal government and it is up to it to provide protection against the unpredictable hazards of life that might occur. The mere failure or inability of the individual to plan for his golden years seems also to be embraced in the concept of the hazardous life.

Those covered by the Social Security System, and now it includes practically everyone by virtue of medicare for non-working participants as well, tacitly agree that the State should assume this responsibility. With the inclusion of physicians the Social Security System as presently constituted is all embracing and is compulsory. Virtually the only group, aside from Government workers, who are not compelled to participate is the clergy. They alone retain the right of election to come in or stay out. The multi-millionaire must be a party to it, even if he has an annual income of a million dollars and by no stretch of the imagination is in danger of becoming a public charge. He too will receive his monthly check regardless of the clear fact that he is not and never will be in need.

The history of the Social Security System in America, as in other countries, started with modest aims and on a modest scale of contributions, coverage and benefits. As is typical with all welfare programs, the pattern has been following a constantly rising scale of contributions and benefits.

The Social Security tax like the income tax seemed quite innocuous at the start. When the income tax started in 1913 a single person with a taxable income of $5,000.00 paid $20.00. Today he pays thirty-five times as much. If the people knew then what they know now it is extremely doubtful that the 16th Amendment to the Constitution would have been passed.

It was not too long before the constitutionality of the Social Security Act came before the Courts. In 1937, in two landmark decisions both the unemployment insurance and old-age retirement benefit programs of the Social Security Act reached the United States Supreme Court. Mr. Justice Cardozo wrote the majority opinions and there were dissenting opinions in both cases. These were parlous times and the United States Supreme Court held much power in vital areas. Witness its overthrow of the NRA in the Schechter "sick chicken" case and the invalidation of the AAA and other New Deal brainstorms.

The reasoning of the Court in both the majority and dissenting opinions is most revealing of the dichotomy in the field of social legislation in America up to that time. The lines were clearly drawn.

The case of *Steward* v. *Davis*, (301 U.S. 548) was decided in favor of the constitutionality of the unemployment insurance feature of the Social Security Act by a 5-4 vote. The case of *Helvering* v. *Davis* (301 U.S. 619) upheld the validity of the old age pension provisions of the Social Security Act by a 7-2 vote.

For the majority of the Court in the Steward case, Mr. Justice Cardozo delivered the opinion in which he justified the Social Security Act under the general welfare clause in the Constitution saying:

"During the years 1929 to 1936, when the country was passing through a cyclical depression, the number of the unemployed mounted to unprecedented heights. Often the average was more than 10 million; at times a peak was attained of 16 million or more. Disaster to the breadwinner meant disaster to dependents. Accordingly the role of the unemployed, itself formidable enough, was only a partial role of the destitute or needy. The fact developed quickly that the states were unable to give the requisite relief. The problem had become national in area and dimensions. There was need of help from the nation if the people were not to starve. It is too late today for the argument to be heard with tolerance that in a crisis so extreme the use of the moneys of the nation to relieve the unemployed and their dependents is a use for any purpose narrower than the promotion of the general welfare." (586-7)

The majority opinion also held that the Social Security Act did not call for a surrender by the states of powers that were essential to their quasi-sovereign existence.

In the Helvering case, the majority of the Supreme Court decided that the old-age pension part of the Social Security Act was constitutional. It called the worker's share of the tax an "income tax on employees" and the other half was designated as "an excise tax on employers". The Circuit Court of Appeals had decided that the "Federal Old-Age Benefits" part of the Social Security Act was void and unconstitutional as an invasion of powers reserved by the Tenth Amendment to the states or to the people, and the Social Security tax likewise void.

The majority of the Court upheld the constitutionality of the Social Security Act and reversed the Circuit Court deciding again that Congress may spend money in aid of the "general welfare"; therefore the taxing and spending for old-age pensions did not contravene the provisions of the Tenth Amendment.

The noble intentions behind the Social Security legislation were stated in the majority opinion of the Court, again written by Justice Cardozo, as follows:

"The hope behind this statute is to save men and women from the rigors of the poorhouse as well as from the haunting fear that such a lot awaits them when journey's end is near."(641)

Justice McReynolds, who dissented in both cases wrote a scholarly opinion in the Steward case in which he reviewed the history of the Union and the doctrine of separability as expressed in the Constitution, under which all powers not delegated to the United States, nor prohibited to the States, are reserved to the States respectively, or to the people. He cited at length and endorsed the opinion of President Franklin Pierce in a veto message to the Senate in 1854 in which he said:

"The question presented, therefore, clearly is upon the constitutionality and propriety of the Federal Government assuming to enter into a novel and vast field of legislation, namely, that of providing for the care and support of all those among the people of the United States who by any form of calamity become fit objects of public philanthropy.

"I readily and, I trust, feelingly acknowledge the duty incumbent on us all as men and citizens, and as among the highest and holiest of our duties, to provide for those who, in the mysterious order of Providence, are subject to want and to disease of body or mind; but I can not find any authority in the Constitution for making the Federal Government the great almoner of public charity throughout the United States. To do so would, in my judgment, be contrary to the letter and spirit of the Constitution and subversive of the whole theory upon which the Union of these States is founded. And if it were admissible to contemplate the exercise of this power for any object whatever, I can not avoid the belief that it would in the end be prejudicial rather than beneficial in the noble offices of charity to have the charge of them transferred from the States to the Federal Government." (602-3)

I have reviewed the opinions in these two cases in depth because of their tremendous importance in pointing the course the country was embarking upon in strengthening the power and authority of the Central Government at the expense of the states and individuals and in giving it a green light in all questions embracing the nebulous, and indistinct "general welfare" of the nation.

However, Social Security was now the law of the land, and when Social Security taxes were first levied in 1937, the maximum tax anyone could have paid was $30.00 per year and the income tax was small besides. Social Security taxes were computed on the basis of 1% on the first $3000.00 of annual wages. It stayed at that rate through 1949. From 1950 on, the base and the rate escalated to the point where in 1969, the first $7800.00 of annual earnings were taxed and at the rate of 4.8% on such earnings from both employee and employer. This already enormous take of 9.6% escalated still further so that starting in 1969 the rate of taxation increased in a series of steps that will take it to 11.8% of the first $7800.00 of annual income in 1987 taxed in equal shares from both employee and employer, and as an educated guess I will venture to predict that the base will rise substantially still further to perhaps $15,000 annually.

Maximum Social Security taxes went up from $30.00 annually when collections began in 1937 to $374.40 thirty three years later or an increase of over 1000 percent. The 1% rate and the taxable base having remained constant until 1950, this tremendous increase was accomplished in only 20 years. Precedent would seem to leave no doubt and it is a sure bet that this trend will continue in the years to come. This, of course, is in addition to federal, state, and in many cases city income taxes plus the thousands of other direct and indirect taxes. Social Security taxes or "contributions," which is the word often euphemistically used to describe them, are, as I shall show, just another form of tax on incomes.

During the last 30 years there has been a hodge-podge of extensive amendments to Social Security in America with no particular adherence to any basic philosophy. These changes were largely the outgrowth of political pressures with too little thought given to the fiscal and economic ramifications involved. One of the aspirants for election to the presidency in 1968 in one of his campaign speeches promised to work for adequate Social Security pensions which he suggested should be at least $100.00 per week for an individual and $150.00 weekly for a married couple.

Another proposed major revision, for example, that seems to be headed for success is that payroll taxes which on the surface are the only source for paying Social Security benefits should not bear the burden alone but that the government should also contribute from its general revenues. One other suggestion is due to the recognition that the "trust fund" from which benefits are theoretically paid is a fiction and should be entirely abolished. Policy makers are now being urged to substitute a pay-as-you go financing method, taking the funds from general revenues as required. The government's taxing power will always guarantee the payment of promised benefits. Basically the recipients are paid benefits out of current production anyway, the "reserve" or "trust fund" fiction notwithstanding. No one suggests that the government promises as outlined in prevailing Social Security schedules will not be met. We can be quite sure that the dollar amounts will be forthcoming on schedule. We can also be just as sure that each year the purchasing power of these dollars will diminish.

All during the 1940s the tax rates were frozen at 1% each for worker and employer despite the fact that they were scheduled to rise to 2% each in 1943, 2½% in 1946, and 3% in 1949. This freezing of the tax contributions ignored the advice of the Commissioner of Social Security, Mr. Altmeyer, who in hearings on the Social Security Administration amendments of 1949 before the 81st Congress said:

> "... this is a system of increasing cost. That is why I favored an increase in contributions the seven times it has come up for consideration before the Committee. ..."

By that time the combined rate should have risen to 6% but it was still 2%. Using Social Security taxes as a fiscal device was the rationale at that time and has been given increased weight since then too. In periods of inflation it is the thinking of the New Economics that the worker should not be trusted to spend or save too much of his wages but should transfer that privilege to his government through an increase in Social Security taxes. However, political pressures seem to go in the opposite direction by giving increased benefits at the same time thus nullifying the anti-inflation reasoning in support of increasing Social Security contributions as a fiscal device.

From time to time Congress has been requested to consider increasing Social Security benefits without a corresponding increase in taxes in order to stimulate consumption during periods of recession in the economy. It was also recognized that Social Security taxes like other taxes are deflationary in their ultimate effect by removing purchasing power from the private sector of the economy.

The original Committee on Economic Security set up by President Roosevelt in 1934 was directed to "study the problems relating to economic security and to make recommendations, both for a long-time and an immediate program of legislation which would promote economic security for the individual." As we have seen the Committee's study resulted first in the public-assistance part of the Social Security Act. It urged however that an insurance program be set up out of which benefits would be paid to relieve the plight of the aged as a long term solution and a dignified substitute for public assistance. It was to be based on joint and equal contributions by both worker and employer with benefits keyed to those contributions and payments guaranteed just like an earned annuity from a private insurance company. The analogy to private insurance was extended by having an account set up on the government records for each taxpayer, contemplating that each worker would get out of the system at least as much as he had paid into it. This feature embraced in the original act was later abandoned.

The majority of the Committee on Economic Security thought that the government should also contribute into the so-called Social Security fund which incidentally was the usual practice adopted by other countries in their Social Security programs. Congress, however, did not go along with the scheme requiring the Government to make contributions along with employee and employer.

In 1956 women were permitted to receive permanently reduced benefits at 62 instead of age 65 when their male counterparts were eligible. In 1961, the retirement age for men at reduced benefits was also lowered to age 62, in both cases at a 20% lifetime reduction. In 1965, this was further reduced as to widows who may now obtain benefits at 60. There have been many other amendments to the Social Security Act of varying importance. One earth shaking amendment provided that earnings from work in the production of turpentine would count toward Social Security benefits starting with January 1, 1959.

One large group received preferential treatment, even though they paid no Social Security taxes. These "workers" were members of the armed services during and after the second World War. For each month of active service between September 1940 and December 1956, they were credited on the records of the Social Security System with earnings of $160.00. Since in fact they had paid nothing, the so-called Social Security trust funds were reimbursed out of general tax collections to that extent. Since 1957, members of the armed forces have been fully covered on a contributory basis. However, since 1968 they have been treated as a specially favored group and aside from their veterans' benefits, they get credit for an additional $100.00 over their base pay, with no Social Security tax deducted on that sum.

Another sizeable class was included in Social Security coverage without the payment of one cent in taxes, either by themselves or in their behalf. In 1966 it was provided that anyone who attained the age of 72 years before 1968 would get a check, by merely establishing his or her age. There are now 3200 people over the age of 100 who are receiving Social Security checks, many of them retired before Social Security even began.

The great extension of Social Security benefits seems endless. The ink is hardly dry on a new amendment before others drop into the legislative hopper. Nobody is ever satisfied despite increases of disbursements of over twentyfold in one decade of Social Security. In thirty five years of the existence of the Social Security System in America, I have not seen or heard of one person whose quest for security was deemed satisfied because of it. Let us then see whether it is an illusion or whether true security lies in another direction.

III

• • • • • • • • •

Social Security at Home and Abroad

ON March 8, 1881, the "Iron Chancellor" Otto von Bismarck, made the first proposal to the German Reichstag for a government health and sickness insurance program. With unusual frankness, very rare in political circles these days, Bismarck urged that his proposal would serve to re-distribute income so as to improve the condition of the "non-propertied classes, which are at the same time the most numerous and the least enlightened".

A health insurance law thereafter went into effect in 1883 in Germany, and old-age and disability laws followed in 1889. It has been suggested that Bismarck was not a humanitarian particularly concerned with the poor, but that his espousal of social insurance was designed to take the steam out of the opposition Social Democratic party which was giving the Hohenzollern monarchy a hard time. The opposition consistently claimed that Social Security was merely a plan of throwing a bone to the workers and was an attempt to bribe them into complacency.

Under Bismarck's plan a reserve fund was set up from

which the retired worker would draw his pension. This accumulation of reserves evaporated when inflation bankrupted the German Government in 1923. Since that time, as under the current American scheme, those now working are paying the old-age pensions of those who are retired.

Under Hitler, the pretense was continued that a pension fund was in operation and that reserves were accumulating just the same as under a true private funding plan administered by an insurance company. Of course, as fast as the tax deductions destined for the social security fund came in, Hitler used them for war purposes and America is doing practically the same thing. The deductions from the workers' pay envelopes, clearly marked "Federal Old Age Tax" and technically so earmarked, actually wind up in the general funds and are used for such things as paying farmers for not producing, foreign aid, etc. Congress then appropriates each year sufficient funds to make the required Social Security payments.

When we add to the foregoing misrepresentations the fact that a worker entering the social security system pays in dollars of one value, and upon retirement gets back dollars of a much reduced value, due principally to inflation caused by the very hand that is supposed to care for him in his old age, we see how he has been tricked and deluded. The security promised him in his old age becomes a mockery.

The tragic and clumsy bungling of a nation's economy by the politicians of Germany after the first World War should be an object lesson for the current breed of government officials both here and abroad. After the war, the German financial wizards thought they could stimulate the economy by inflating the money supply and by deficit financing, and thus revive the stagnating economy, and create full employment. Of course, they planned it only to be a small inflation, just enough to do the trick and it was to be under the complete control of the astute managers.

The resulting uncontrollable inflation utterly destroyed the value of the Social Security System in Germany and pensioners could not buy one egg with their monthly check. Chaos wracked that devastated land, registered unemployment between 1928 and 1932 rising from 650,000 to over six million, thus planting the seeds for Hitler and the next World War.

The following chart from a German history book (*Um Volksstaat and Volkergemeinschaft* published by Ernst Klett, Stuttgart, 1961, page 149) graphically portrays the inflation which ended in the bankruptcy of the German government in 1923.

PRICES IN GERMANY (*in Marks*)

	1914	1918	1922	1923 Summer	1923 November
Potatoes (pound)	.04	.12	80	2,000	50,000,000,000
Egg (one)	.08	.25	180	5,000	80,000,000,000
Beer (Glass)	.13	.17	60	3,000	150,000,000,000
Meat (pound)	.90	2.00	1,200	90,000	3,200,000,000,000
Butter (pound)	1.40	3.00	2,400	150,000	6,000,000,000,000

After this debacle, the Hitler regime went through the motions of accumulating a "Trust Fund" for old-age pensions, but as in America it was quickly diverted to other uses, principally for re-arming.

Germany has not been alone in suffering the devastating effects of inflation. In Brazil, for example, an annual depreciation in the purchasing power of the cruzeiro of 35% and more, is considered normal.

In France, at the end of the second World War, the franc was worth just one-twenty fifth as much as in 1914. By 1950, a fixed monthly income from Social Security and other funds, which might have supported a pensioner in 1914, would buy one meal a month. In just 36 years, the French franc lost more than 99% of its purchasing power. It is quite clear why the French people's penchant is strong for keeping their gold in mattresses at home rather than converting it into francs or dollars in banks.

France now automatically adjusts Social Security pensions in response to changes in the official price or wage index. Belgium, Chile, Denmark, Ecuador, Finland, Israel, Luxemborg, The Netherlands, Sweden and Uruguay also provide for such adjustments, thus attempting to overcome the harmful effects of inflation, but it just doesn't work. In America, the adjustment is not automatic, but periodic. The only way these promises of something for nothing can work is to pay-off in cheaper coin of the realm.

Before the end of his first year in office, President Nixon proposed tying Social Security benefits to the cost of living. This represented a major departure from past policy which was to increase benefits generally during election years. In making his proposal for such automatic escalation of benefits, Mr. Nixon said that a prime reason for his doing so was "to depoliticize, to a certain extent, the Social Security System and give a greater stability to what has become a cornerstone of our society's social insurance system." As Nixon put it, this would "make certain once and for all that the retired, the disabled and the dependent never again bear the brunt of inflation." The automatic cost-of-living benefit adjustments would be made annually based upon increases in the Labor Department's index of consumer prices. His proposal provides for automatic increases in the maximum amount of the wage base on which Social Security taxes are paid in order to pay for any such benefit increase. This wage base escalation would take place every second year and not annually as the benefits increased. A wage base then in a few years of $15,000 subject to Social Security taxes under this plan would not be entirely a shocker.

There are now over one hundred countries that have a social security program. Since the establishment of a social security system of one sort or another in these countries, the pattern has been one of constantly increasing benefits and taxes, just as in the United States. Neither is ever reduced.

All of the countries in both Western and Eastern Europe have some form of statutory old-age disability and survivor benefit program and throughout the rest of the world, it has become a status symbol of an emerging country to at least have a social security system if it cannot afford the luxury of a national airline, or a steel mill, both generally heavily subsidized.

Until America joined up with its plan of a pension to everyone at age 72, regardless of need, or whether or not the worker contributed to a retirement plan or ever worked, there were at least seven other countries that beat the United States to the gun in that respect: Canada, Denmark, Finland, Iceland, New Zealand, Norway, and Sweden gave pensions to every non-contributing resident above a specified age. Some countries require citizenship as a prerequisite to qualify for benefits, others merely require residence therein for varying periods. In some countries, pensions are not paid to aliens while residing out of the country. In some countries retirement is necessary, others not. There are also plans, as in the United States, where partial retirement is permitted. For some mysterious reason, utterly devoid of logic, the United States, among other countries, does not insist on retirement after a more advanced age in order to qualify, to wit 72, and attaches no penalty to such earnings. There are many countries, among them Canada, France, West Germany, and Switzerland, that do not impose any general retirement condition, and pay full pensions even though the recipient is employed full time and chooses to continue working. In some countries both residence and citizenship are required unless a reciprocity agreement is in effect with the country in which the retiree is domiciled. There are all sorts of varying benefits for widows and orphans and it is not within the scope of this study to compare or analyze the many different systems in great detail.

In theory, in America, Social Security benefits are paid because the wage-earner has put aside part of his wages as a fund out of which retirement benefits will be received by him in his non-productive old age. This is pure fiction and as I will establish in the following pages bears no relationship at all to the facts. What the Social Security System accomplishes is merely to transfer money from the pay envelopes of the working population into the hands of those who cannot work or who by law are dissuaded from working because they are old or disabled or who are entitled to monthly checks because they fit the definition of "dependents" arbitrarily fixed by statute.

A non-working millionaire living all his life on income from investments may also qualify for Social Security benefits in America. This can be accomplished by making one of his investments, and a relatively small one at that, in an interest in oil or gas properties which will yield him a net income of at least $400.00 per year. His working interest in a producing well which can represent an insignificant fraction of the total ownership of the property will be managed by professionals. Income so derived is treated by the Treasury as "self-employment income" and is taxed just as wages, thus qualifying him for all Social Security benefits.

There is no reason why this "self-employment income" necessarily has to come from an interest in gas or oil. An interest as proprietor or partner is any business or profession, including farming can do the trick in America. The source and extent of the contributions and the administrative organizations handling the collections and the benefits also vary from country to country. In general, however, there have been established separate Social Security Institutes, Administrations, Boards, or Organizations to handle the programs.

Many plans include maternity benefits too. In England, for example, cash maternity benefits are payable for 11 weeks before and 7 weeks after confinement, in addition to a lump sum maternity grant. While the United States is laggard in this respect, it is bound to catch up in due time. Presently only two states in the United States pay maternity benefits. In Rhode Island the maternity benefit is 55% of earnings for a maximum of 14 weeks and in New Jersey 61% to 67% of earnings payable for a period not to exceed 8 weeks.

As pointed out before, from the time of Bismarck in 1889, and continuing right up to the present time, the German worker's welfare and security have been a prime concern of the state. In 1965, West Germany's social welfare budget was about sixteen billion dollars, two-thirds of which was financed by contributions of employers and employees for old-age pensions and unemployment, health, and accident insurance. The balance of the tab was picked up directly by the Government of West Germany out of general tax collections. There are special allowances to some families with two children and to all families with three or more.

England, too, has been another modern state which has gone all out on the cradle to the grave philosophy for its citizens including all sorts of expanding health measures embodied in the typical socialized medicine program.

In Canada and in some other foreign countries, the governments provide minimum subsistence payments to all eligible persons regardless of other income.

Extensive Social Security legislation was enacted in Russia after World War I. In the Soviet Union all who have worked 20 to 25 years receive old age pensions from age 45 to 60 years, depending on their classification or work. The Soviet worker contributes nothing toward his pension and if his skill and services are in demand he receives the same amount even though he continues to work after reaching his age limit. The introduction of this provision in 1964 increased the percentage of working old-age pensioners from 9.4% to 14% by 1966. Various socialist countries including Russia impose charges for some welfare services.

In the United States, Social Security legislation came relatively late. Before World War II most European nations had already adopted old-age insurance and many of them also provided disability and survivor benefits. A principal reason for America's being laggard in this respect was that the American economy was basically agricultural, the western frontier still beckoned and the ambitious could still make a living by heeding Horace Greeley's advice. Land if not free, was still relatively cheap and if you had access to land and were willing to work, you had security.

When, however, these conditions no longer prevailed, work for wages became the order of the day, and depressions became more severe and prolonged. Urban real estate became very expensive to buy or rent. Land speculation was rampant and land was held out of use. Speculative rent that was exacted exceeded true economic rent so that the entrepeneur was of necessity doomed to bankruptcy.

Because of these new problems which came later to America only because it was younger, the United States followed the older European nations in attempting to protect its people from the economic hazards that seemed to be part of a maturing nation.

Peculiarly, the expanding welfare state has brought neither security or peace to this troubled world. The governments with the greatest welfare programs have been more or less constantly at war or preparing for it. Of all the major countries, the German Federal Republic ranks highest in annual Social Security expenditures per capita. In 1960 the latest year for which comparative material is available, West Germany spent $195.00 per capita, the lowest being India with $1.00. ("The Cost of Social Security", Geneva International Labor Office 1964) From Bismarck's time on, there has been no security or peace for the German people and it took the second World War and Hitler to solve Germany's unemployment problem. Perhaps the war gave them more security than peace, since the Fuehrer promised them a future free of problems in the Greater Reich.

England high up on the list of countries with high per capita Social Security is most insecure as of the present writing despite decades of expanding social security. Austerity measures have been interposed and notwithstanding massive injections of foreign loans and assistance from the World Bank, the pound was devalued and is likely to be further devalued.

In America, with one of the largest per capita Social Security expenditures, there is no security either. The worker is insecure in his job and strikes and marches on Washington are the order of the day. In the cities where the welfare programs are the thickest, there are race riots and increasing crime rates, and anti-poverty programs proliferate.

In France, where an employer alone pays a 30% payroll tax

and a worker 6%, a married worker can keep on working after 60 and still collect 30% of his salary as a pension and at 65 the pension can go up to 60%. Health payments in France cover 80% of all medical and dental expenses for young and old alike. There is a sick-pay benefit and a family allowance which can add 50% of a man's pay. When Andre Malraux became de Gaulle's Minister of Culture he even arranged for social security benefits for his country's artists. In 1967 despite severe opposition France took an unusual step in the history of Social Security legislation and reformed its Social Security law including a slash in medical benefits. The share of workers medical bills paid by Social Security dropped from 80 per cent to 70. This was done in an attempt to stem the rising costs and the inflationary tide but it was not long before the workers responded with strikes to the reduction and in hundreds of idle factories placards were raised demanding restoration of the cuts in medical benefits under Social Security, more generous allowances, higher wages, better prices for the farmers, and de Gaulle's head to boot. There was a social security deficit of 3.4 billion francs or $677 million dollars at the end of 1967, largely due to the sickness insurance program. The government proposed reform brought a storm of protest from the labor unions and to a lesser extent from management as well, both fearing the loss of purchasing power. The Government stood firm for a while but after the social crisis of May 1968 it backed down and substantially restored the cuts. Social Security expenditures in France in 1967 reached 60% of the regular budget and about 14% of the gross national product.

In West Germany, sick pay gives a worker 85% of his salary. Young and old have most of their medical expenses paid. The medical benefits even include an annual trip to a spa with $2 a day pocket money.

These European governments are able to pay benefits like these because their social security programs are, in effect, welfare programs. Not only do employers and employees contribute to the various social security plans, but the governments also chip in. In America we have recently openly started to do the same thing with the money coming from general tax revenues in order to pay pensions to non-contributors at age 72. There are Congressmen here too who would like to match or outdo in generosity their European counterparts particularly in election years.

In giving pensions to non-contributors at 72 in 1966, America has finally gone the way of other countries who have made a distinction between universal old-age pensions stressing fixed adequacy payments which generally have a much lower ceiling, and pension benefits keyed to earnings.

As far back as 1952 Canada gave all its senior citizens, rich and poor alike, a fixed amount merely because they attained the required age. This was financed by surcharges on the individual and corporation income taxes, and manufacturers sales tax. Like its American counterpart, the Canada Pension Plan, effective in 1965, added a social insurance plan financed by equal contributions from both worker and employer. Self-employed are also covered but pay the entire combined tax. Under the Canadian system the individual's social security taxes are deductible for income tax purposes, but benefits are considered ordinary taxable income when received. Canada uses a system of family allowances which gives parents $72- to $120- per year for each child according to his or her age.

In discussions of the pros and cons of the Welfare State, Sweden is generally cited as a prime example of what a beneficent semi-socialist state can do and has done for its citizens. What is overlooked, however, are some very significant facts and figures that the admirers of the Swedish system conveniently neglect to mention.

In the dozen or so years prior to 1960 the share of social welfare expenditures as a proportion of the gross national product increased from about 8% to 14%. Now these welfare expenditures represent 37% of all government expenses and compulsory health insurance, inaugurated in 1955, alone amounts to more than one-third of all these welfare disbursements. Despite the fact that in Sweden about 70% of the entire population was already insured in private voluntary health plans the compulsory scheme was made effective as of January 1, 1955, traceable as a political issue among the Social Democrats and the Conservatives, as well as other political parties.

For the decade before that date, 1945–1955, the number of reported illnesses per 100 privately insured members remained virtually fixed, running between 30 to 32%. Within a few years under the government operated complusory plan the rate went up to 55%.

Of course when Sweden is cited so approvingly by the admirers of the welfare state, they manage to ignore the crippling cost in direct income and other taxes. A married couple earning the equivalent of $3,000 must pay 27% of their earned income over that up to $5,000. When they reach the $5,000 bracket they pay 42% on the excess and then their tax escalates upwards still further.

In exchange for this heavy tax burden, almost every conceivable social benefit has been provided for starting before birth. The Swedish woman, married or not, receives free pre- and post-natal care including free dental services during her pregnancy and for 270 days after delivery. When baby comes, she is provided with free hospital services plus a cash payment of $175.00. This cash payment is an annual payment for each child. These extensive benefits continue for the aged as well as for the young, and include even free foot-care for tired old legs.

The relative economic stability of Sweden can be attributed to many causes other than the advent and aggrandizement of the welfare state. She is richly endowed with natural resources, has remained neutral in recent wars and her citizens are industrious, intelligent, and skillful. In addition, the attitude of Swedish labor unions towards the capitalist is quite enlightened. The president of the leading organization of about 40 industrial unions, with about 20% of the entire population, Arne Geijer, recently commented: "A company's profitability and its ability to pay wages are closely connected. Therefore, it's a union necessity to show interest in a company's internal efficiency, as well as conditions for the workers."

However, despite its economic security, Sweden is far from per capita affluence, has an increasing crime rate, particularly among its youth, alcoholism is widespread, the suicide rate is high, and life there has been described as quite dull and uninteresting.

In Italy in 1969 after three months of recurring general strikes, the government and the four largest labor unions finally reached an agreement increasing pensions and modifying certain Social Security reform measures promulgated the year before by a newly installed government.

Throughout the world, the pattern of increasing benefits is the rule and any government that appears to be niggardly finds itself in trouble. The Italian Government had decided that the increased level of benefit in the 1968 law represented the maximum it could grant consistent with the state of the economy. The union negotiators argued otherwise and felt the increase was inadequate after a lapse of 3½ years from the last raise in benefits and did not make up for the rise in the cost of living over that period. The unions were vehement also in advocating repeal of the provision in the 1968 law reducing or eliminating pensions for workers over 65 who elected to continue working. This provision is still the law in the United States. In Italy under the new law, earnings will not disqualify a pensioner's right to his old-age pension if he is 65 or more. The new law in Italy also provides for automatic adjustments in pension payments keyed to increases in the cost of living. Incidentally, both Nixon and Humphrey campaigning for the presidency in 1968, also supported automatic increases in Social Security benefits tied to escalation in the cost of living. However after the election, Robert H. Finch, Nixon's Secretary of Health, Education, and Welfare told a Congressional Committee he did not favor automatic cost-of-living adjustments on the ground of sound financing.

An editorial in the *New York Times* of May 8, 1969, entitled "Retreat on Social Security" commented on this apparent change of heart as follows:

In a time of inflation, the worst victims are elderly persons living on pensions. The economy may be booming to new highs, but their income does not change. Recognizing the painful bite higher prices take out of their limited purchasing power both parties last year promised to tie Social Security payments to the cost of living. Like all such escalator provisions, this proposal has the disadvantage of tending to aggravate the inflation it is designed to offset. But it is unfair for a Government that is failing to hold the value of the dollar steady to deny relief to those hardest hit by rising prices.

Since the election, both parties have been steadily retreating from this pledge. Officials of the new Administration dismissed an escalator clause as too expensive. President Nixon cut back the increase of Social Security benefits recommended by President Johnson from 10% to 7% to save a billion dollars in the budget, but he retained the proposed increase in Social Security taxes.

Illustrative of the fact that Social Security payments in America as well as in other countries are not like benefits provided for in an insurance policy, is the power of the government to unilaterally alter the terms of the so-called "contract". A worker may think he has a legally enforceable claim to his Social Security benefit but he is under a delusion if he does. Congress has merely been making a gift to him which future Congresses may modify or even revoke entirely. The United States Supreme Court has in fact ruled that Social Security payments when received are not taxable income but are actually gifts and are not like income received from paid up insurance policies or annuity contracts which is taxable.

America adhered to the general view that the right to benefits was earned and paid for by the worker and therefore the beneficiary's place of residence should have no bearing on his right to receive payment wherever he chose to reside thereafter. However, the Social Security Amendments of 1967, effective July 1, 1968, made some significant changes altering and suspending payment of benefits to non-citizens of the United States living abroad. So we see that it is just a question of "Promises, Promises", and one of the "contracting" parties can change the "contract" without the consent of the other both here and abroad. This is not to suggest however that any government anywhere will seriously and substantially diminish the level of Social Security benefits. The political consequences would be too horrible for them to contemplate.

Reference to these varied social security systems is made to illustrate that there is not much novelty in any one of them nor have they fulfilled the aims outlined in the preambles to the legislative findings which launched them on their way.

The ostensible justification for all the compulsory social security systems was that without them the individual in general would be powerless to provide for himself in his old age in this complex society. It therefore became the presumptive duty of the State to adopt some method of accomplishing for the individual what was obviously good for him, but which for various reasons more or less beyond his control he could not or would not provide for himself. He would not have the ability nor the will to make intelligent decisions with regard to how to save for his retirement.

The rationale was that in the end this compulsion would relieve the State of the burden of administering the public dole and would dignify the individual's acceptance of Social Security payments when he was no longer productive instead of putting him on the relief rolls. The analogy with a private insurance policy funding a true pension plan was thus clearly outlined, the only difference being that the element of compulsion was introduced in order to make it effective.

Unfortunately, Social Security has not abolished or even reduced the relief rolls. Peculiarly, insecurity seems to be a concomitant of expanding social security.

Since security does not come hand in hand with the increasing role of the Welfare State, is it obtainable, and if so, how? People everywhere are constantly searching for Utopia, trying to discover some panacea that will guarantee their security and establish the Good Society all over the world. The current vehicle designed to carry us into the promised land is a greatly expanded Social Security System.

IV

• • • • • • • •

Social Security Semantics

FROM the beginning of time, the search for security has always been present in the minds of men. The production of weapons was part of that craving as was community life itself. This striving for security is a strong animal instinct. Man, from the stone age on, as distinguished from other animals, seeks to attain his economic security by storing wealth in the form of tools or machinery as capital goods, not to be immediately consumed but to be used by him or loaned to others in order to produce more efficiently. This, they discovered, would enable the producers to stock pile some wealth for a rainy day, or lend the capital to some one else in return for interest, which is only payment for the use of capital which enables the borrower to produce more and retain more things for himself. Security is thereby attained in that fashion for the lender and borrower both of whom are now wealthier. This follows the truism that man seeks to satisfy his desires with the least effort.

Unforeseen hazards and tragedies increased with the complexity of modern civilization, and the institution of the private insurance company was born. The purpose was to organize a system of protection against loss through a sharing of the risk whereby a number of individuals agreed to pay certain sums for a guarantee that they would be compensated for any specified loss caused by fire, accident, death, or any other disaster sought to be insured against. Private insurance companies would be able to back up this guarantee by making reasonably accurate projections of future costs of indemnification when disaster struck their policyholders and then levy a charge or premium on each member of the group. This would provide the money conservatively estimated to be sufficient to reimburse those who might suffer the loss insured against and at the same time cover all administrative expenses including a return on the capital invested in the insurance company.

In all the millions of Social Security pamphlets and brochures published and distributed by the Social Security Administration the word "insurance" plays a prominent role. However, while the Social Security program deceptively carries the aura of stability and fiscal soundness established over the centuries by insurance companies, it is in no way circumscribed by any of the rules and regulations to which private insurance companies are subject. For example, private companies as we have seen must set aside reserves out of which claim payments will ultimately be made so that there will be no danger of default even if new business slackens or in the unlikely event the company decides to liquidate. In buying private insurance today the individual doesn't even give a thought to investigating the solvency of the company so assured is he in that regard. The Social Security System however doesn't have to maintain any real reserves or be bound by sound actuarial principles or have to prove its solvency. This is generally recognized in foreign practices where normally the Government participates. After all, the Government's taxing power is a fine substitute for a reserve fund.

In this connection the Advisory Council on Economic Security, which is appointed every five years, in its report in 1948 said:

"In our opinion, the cost of financing the accrued liability should not be met solely from the payroll contributions of employers and employees. We believe that this burden would more properly be borne at least in part, by the general revenues of the government."

However when Congress amended the Social Security Act in 1950 it rejected the idea of a government contribution and this, although already modified to some extent, is still the basic law today despite subsequent amendments and revisions of many kinds.

The Social Security System was adopted during the most severe depression America ever experienced, when a tremendous number of the country's able-bodied men were out of work through no fault of their own and were ready, willing, and able to take virtually any job at all. The term "Social Insurance" came into general use since it was found that private insurance companies did not insure against these particular economic hazards of life. The Federal Government got into the business for the ostensible purpose of insuring against the hazards of old-age, contemplating that the elderly would have no funds or income with which to provide for their needs. Concern for the jobless and the aged poor has involved the Federal Government more and more since the adoption of the Social Security Act. This has followed the growing conviction that it is the duty of the central government rather than the individual himself to provide for his old age, since it appeared clear that laissez faire economics of pre Social Security times failed so miserably.

Of course there are millions of people who have provided for their old age and have even bought life insurance as a means of taking care of their loved ones in the event of death during their productive years. By a large margin, Americans own more life insurance than all the rest of the world put together. About one-fifth of all people who have reached 65 years of age and over are now getting pensions from private sources. It is estimated that almost one-half of them by the year 1980 will be getting an income through private pension plans. In addition millions of younger people have also bought private insurance to protect and provide for a continuance of their income in the event of disabling accident or illness.

Those who support a compulsory social insurance plan under the aegis of the Federal Government, say that given the hazards of existence under the capitalistic system, the individual is either too stupid, too helpless or doesn't care enough about providing for himself and that anyway the State is better qualified. They contend that if the government didn't take over this job, those who are intelligent and fore-sighted enough to make private provision for escaping the impact of these hazards, would in the long run also have to bear the burden and expense of those who don't care, or don't have the means or brains to protect themselves during the lean years.

Somehow, in some mysterious fashion the masses are deemed wise enough to vote into office those other individu-als presumably much smarter than they are who will take care of them and to delegate to them that duty and obligation rather than worry and attempt to do what they can about it themselves. This is analogous to the situation where the State passes anti-gambling laws apparently to prevent these same masses from being fools and losing all their hard earned money. After all, it declares that it is only restricting their freedom for their own good. Nevertheless, the State sees nothing wrong if the same mass man makes a jackass of himself going broke at a race-track provided it is duly licensed by the State and from which the State gets a cut. Gambling is also sanctioned if the State conducts a lottery, otherwise the same state of facts becomes a crime.

The advertising genius who came up with the promotional slogan "Fair Trade" for price fixing under various government protective policies guaranteeing monopolies, had nothing on the creative genius who got the Social Security System to use the word "insurance" in the title "Old Age, Survivors & Disability Insurance" now used to describe the Social Security System. Politicians have a facility for falsifying and distorting the normal meaning of words in order to make them serve their political ends.

In 1968 a pamphlet was issued by the Brookings Institution entitled "The Objectives of Social Security". Its three authors were respectively the director of economics studies of Brookings and professors of economics at the University of Maryland and Rutgers. The authors acknowledged that Social Security had an appealing but distorted image based on "a misleading analogy to private insurance". They observed "In practice as well as in principle—Social Security is not a substitute for private insurance, but rather a mechanism for transferring financial resources from the working generation to those who cannot work because of age, disability, or dependency status. This is a point that has been emphasized by many economists and is no longer in serious dispute."

Nevertheless, the Social Security Administration persists in perpetuating this myth. It gets so absorbed in the barrage of propaganda which it pours out, that it has even gone so far as to produce regular half hour programs for TV to prove how wonderful it is to get a monthly check from the government. It shows those happy dear old faces, so appreciative of the largesse bestowed upon them smiling to you across your TV screen now enjoying their golden years because of the "insurance" thoughtfully provided by the State. The poor bedraggled and ulcer-ridden taxpayer who slaves all his working life to help pay for the pittance the kindly old folks are shown receiving on TV and who in addition pays for the cost of producing the TV program, never gets any credits. However, at the beginning and end of the program, as well as at various intermediate spots, due credits are given to the generous Social Security Administration.

Terminology customarily employed in the field of private insurance has been falsely adopted to describe the operation of the Social Security System and is used to palm it off as just another insurance program providing annuities through the Government instead of through private insurance companies. Witness for example the following typical statement by Robert M. Ball , Commissioner of Social Security. [S.S. Bulletin vol. 29, No. 6—June 1966 pp. 3–4]

> The idea [of social security] is simply that while people work and are earning they contribute a part of their earnings to a fund, with contributions from the employer and now, in many countries, also from the Government. When earnings stop because one is too old to work or too disabled to work or because the wage earner in the family dies or because there is no job to be had or there are extra expenses connected with illness, for example, then the accumulated funds from all contributors are used to make up for the loss of income or to meet, in part or in whole, the expenses incurred. In return for setting aside some of the money one has when one is earning,

the system provides an assured income when one is not. Social insurance, like all insurance, averages out among all who are covered the risk that is too much for any one individual to bear.

The speciousness of this analogy is obvious by citing a simple case. For example if John Doe had paid the maximum into his so-called Social Security account, at age 65 when he retires, he might get $150.00 monthly. His cousin Richard Roe who started to work at the same time, also earned the maximum subject to Social Security and he too retired at 65. Richard however now gets $225.00 monthly instead of the $150.00 John gets. How Come? Simple. John is a bachelor, Richard's wife is 65 also. Under private insurance, of course they would be treated exactly alike. The same premiums would buy the same annuity.

What the Government has done in the above case and in others like those for instance where it has decided to give everyone over 72 a pension, even if he didn't pay 5¢ worth of premiums, is merely to redistribute income in an arbitrary way.

In an unguarded moment, Social Security Chairman Dr. Arthur J. Altmeyer, in a CBS radio interview, frankly admitted this to be its purpose when he said:

> The people with larger incomes and larger resources ought to contribute for the people with the lower income and resources. While it is important to maintain financing [of Social Security] on a basis that insures adequacy of benefits and adaptability of the benefits to income loss, it is also important to make sure that we accomplish something by way of distribution of welfare among the various economic groups of this country, through *a redistribution of some of the income and resources.*

This ephemeral resemblance to true insurance was thoroughly exposed by Barbara Wootton as far back as 1955.

> At this point, the simple facts of the situation are that benefits on a prescribed scale have been promised, and that funds must be provided to meet them; that is all. In these circumstances, the allocation of precise fractions of contributors' payments to cover particular risks becomes an academic, rather than a genuinely actuarial, exercise. The performance of this exercise in the sacred name of insurance demands, however, elaborate and expensive systems of recording the experience of millions of beneficiaries. These monumental systems are indeed a tribute to the skill and accuracy of the administrators who devise them, and to the ingenuity of the mechanical devices employed in their operation; but are they really necessary, and have they, indeed, any meaning? Is it, in fact maintaining what has become no more than a facade? ["The Impact of Income Security on Individual Freedom," in James E. Russell (ed), *National Policies for Education, Health, and Social Services* (Doubleday, 1955) pp. 386–387]

To ask the question is to answer it. The facade is preserved because it serves to dupe the poor suffering taxpayer.

He is also recognized as a puzzled taxpayer in one of the hundreds of booklets printed by the Social Security Administration. (OASI–93 August 1965 p. 21) Apparently some naive ones have asked

"WHY FULL BENEFITS FOR PEOPLE WHO RETIRE NOW?"

and the answer came back:

> "Some people ask why it is that people who have worked under social security for only a few years can retire and get

benefits which may amount to much more than they have paid in taxes.

Remember that these people have had precisely the same loss of earnings as those who will retire after a full lifetime of work under the system."

Well maybe it's not really an earned annuity but they need the money too! And if you are confused its only because you think too much and ask too many questions.

The general principle behind the Social Security System is to take money from all who work either for salaries or for themselves, and pay over certain sums to the elderly, such sums having absolutely no relation to the wealth of the recipient. There are many cases of corporation presidents earning over $100,000.00 per year and at the same time getting Social Security checks. While the government still persists in calling it an insurance system, in effect as we have seen it is a welfare program involving a redistribution of income through the political process. The beneficiaries in the early years of Social Security received much more in benefits than they paid in taxes. Those who contributed for over twenty-five years and are retiring from now on will receive a great deal less than they have paid in. As for new workers just entering the Social Security System they are assuming the great burden of paying the present beneficiaries. Those poor Peters entering the work pool, are now being robbed to pay the Pauls who are retired. The contributions of the retirees have already been spent, and government I.O.U.s in the form of bonds have been substituted almost entirely for their contributions.

Those presently employed hope and implicitly expect that when their retirement day comes, the younger workers will acknowledge a moral obligation to pay them a pension because they did the same for their ancestors. It may dawn on those who are now retiring that they have no "Social Security trust fund" saved up or invested for them to draw against. But if the Government fooled them, shouldn't the younger generation submit to being fooled too? Must a deception once practiced be forever condoned and perpetuated? Perhaps the younger generation is rebelling at the prospect of being taxed for 40 years to pay for someone else's old age pension without even being afforded the courtesy of being asked whether they mind doing so.

Social Security Administration officials and actuaries within and outside of Social Security now concede that only from current and future contributions plus the tapping of general tax receipts can present Social Security pensions be paid. This, of course, is the great difference between private pension plans administered by private insurance companies and Social Security. If private insurance companies do not sell one more policy, and decide to go out of business, actuarily speaking, they will meet all the pension obligations that they contractually entered into to. However, if the Social Security System were terminated, there would be no funds with which to pay the accrued obligations. The receipts were spent in short order and those who had paid into a so-called "trust fund" all their working lives would find that the "trust" fund is full of I.O.U.s of a most hopelessly bankrupt promisor or "insurance company" with only enough assets (cash & U.S. Government securities) to make payments for about one year.

One official of the Social Security Administration says "Continued general support for the Social Security System hinges on continued public ignorance of how the system works." He was frank enough to add: "I believe that we have nothing to worry about because it is so enormously complex that nobody is going to figure it out." (*Barron's Weekly* 4/26/65)

The literature from Washington, is self-laudatory. The increasing benefits are always high-lighted, the increased cost rarely mentioned. Often the science of semantics is employed to camouflage and to deceive. This is flagrantly so when the words "trust funds" and "insurance" are used again and again. For example, Robert J. Myers, the Chief Actuary of the Social Security Administration has said

> "It is recognized that the use of the term 'social insurance' may result in some misunderstanding of the basic nature of a social security program by the general public, who will tend to think of it in terms of their acquaintance and knowledge of private insurance . . . ." [*Social Insurance & Allied Government Programs*—Irwin, 1965 p. 8]

The Government does all it can to perpetuate such misunderstanding.

The growing burden of cost is ignored when related to benefits promised, nor is the constantly diminishing purchasing power of the retirement dollar mentioned. Actually the mushrooming of governmental promises of future delivery is a form of current taxation—a method of dipping into private savings, which winds up as an inflationary device being the basis for the creation of more money. When the government sells one of its bonds, or collects the Social Security tax, it obtains a given amount of real purchasing power from individuals. History has shown us all over the world that the dollars, or pounds or cruzeiros, with which governments eventually redeem their promises lose purchasing power in proportion to the volume of such outstanding promises. Meanwhile, all other promises which are payable in dollars, or coin of the realm, including the obligations of individuals in the usual course of business, also lose their purchasing power. This encourages private spending and discourages saving and private capital formation. Inflation is a subtle and destructive method of taxation and the Social Security System is a part of that destruction of private enterprise in America and throughout the world.

Nevertheless the promises of big government mount in intensity particularly in an election year. After the promise has been enacted into law, it is still a promise whether backed by a bond, or by a social security account. To cancel or destroy the bonds or I.O.U.'s held in the social security fund would not affect the worker's pension when it is due to be paid. The so-called "social security fund" is a joke anyway, since it amounts to less than 1% of today's accrued liability. The promise of a social security pension has value only because the government will be presumed to exercise the power of taxation—not because it has issued bonds. Since the Government will always have the power to tax, the Social Security dollars will be paid, with no representation or guarantee however as to their value or purchasing power. The voting power of the beneficiaries is too immense to even contemplate a default. The ramifications and the effects of making good on the promises however have long been neglected and are in sad need of an airing.

The original Social Security System in 1935 established an old-age annuity program which would pay retired workers at 65 an income for the rest of their lives without a means test and was called Old Age Insurance. When the 1939 amendments to the Social Security System were enacted it became Old Age & Survivors Insurance, and provided protection for the retired worker's family also. In 1954 the risk of disability was also covered and it became known as the Old Age, Survivors, & Disability Insurance (OASDI) program. The word "insurance" is always incorporated in the title. In this way the Social Security System has capitalized on the tremendous good will and prestige that private insurance companies have developed over several centuries. Through the establishment of a fictional "reserve fund", Social Security has placed itself in the category of private insurance companies that are funded on an actuarily sound basis and with adequate reserves to cover virtually all contingencies. The undisputed fact is that the soundness of the entire Social Security System rests not at all on the Social Security Reserve Fund but only upon the power of the government to tax as it goes and to borrow when it is compelled to or when it chooses.

The Federal Government distributes many millions of pamphlets on Social Security. In one series of them entitled "Insurance for You and Your Family", at p. 11, it says:

> Your account number on your social security card identifies your old-age and survivor insurance account. Your card is the symbol of your insurance policy under the Federal Social Security Law.

However in the case of *Helvering* v. *Davis* (301 U.S. 619) the United States Supreme Court had to decide the issue of the constitutionality of the Social Security Act. In the brief filed with the Court by the Government's attorneys in support of its position that the Social Security Act was constitutional the specific point was unequivocally made that

> "The benefits under Title II [Social Security Act] are like pensions, to be given or withheld in the discretion of Congress".

Can you imagine an insurance policy, where after the policy-holder pays the agreed upon premiums and is not in default, the insurance company retains the right to renege on paying off at its sole discretion?

When I went to school, an insurance policy was a contract. I made a deal with a company on certain terms and conditions. Neither of us could unilaterally cancel or modify the insurance contract. Any resemblance of my "insurance policy under the Federal Social Security Law" to an insurance policy in the normal sense of the word is purely fictitious and the statement suggesting any similarity is fraudulent. There is no actual government reserve fund which every private insurance company must maintain on an actuarilly sound basis in order to be licensed to do business. The ability of the Federal Government to make good on its Social Security promises rests on nothing but its power to tax when the time comes to pay off.

The false impression is thus conveyed that this "Social insurance" is similar to private insurance with the same general format of premiums and benefits basic to actuarilly sound private insurance, the only change being that the government is now cast in the role of the private insurance company.

Insurance companies historically, have been licensed and closely regulated by governmental authorities and have won the confidence of the American people. Severe penalties are imposed on violators of the various insurance laws and regulations. Misrepresentations and misleading statements are generally penal offenses, subjecting officers and directors to criminal punishment.

But the double standard seems to apply. Government Social Security literature makes many false and misleading statements, which if made by directors or officers of private insurance companies would result in jail sentences for them. For example the public has been told and is led to believe that the Social Security taxes now being paid in ever-increasing amounts by both employer and employee are put into a separate fund out of which future benefits are to be paid.

In the *Helvering* v. *Davis* case I just cited, the United States Supreme Court succinctly observed in deciding for constitutionality of the Social Security Act as follows:

> "The proceeds of both taxes are to be paid into the Treasury like internal-revenue taxes generally, and are not earmarked in any way."

This was changed by Congress in the 1939 Amendment to the Social Security Act and the elaborate fiction of a trust fund was then created but the handling of the funds in essence remained the same, the only difference being that the Government put its I.O.U. into the "trust fund" when it used the money for its general purposes.

The Social Security Administration of the Department of Health, Education, and Welfare puts out a twenty-four page pamphlet (OASI-93 August 1964) entitled "Your Social Security Earning Record". On page "5" of that booklet the following statement is made.

> The basic idea of old-age, survivors, and disability insurance is a simple one. During working years, employees, their employers, and self-employed people pay social security taxes which go into *trust funds*. Then, when earnings stop because of the worker's retirement in old age, his disability, or his death, payments are made *from the funds* to the worker and his dependents or to his survivors.

On pages 17 and 18 it continues:

> The money to pay old-age, survivors and disability insurance benefits come from social security taxes. It does not come from general taxation. *Under the law*, the money collected as social security taxes can be used *only* to pay social security benefits and the costs of administering the old-age, survivors and disability insurance program.
>
> Money not immediately needed for benefit payments and administrative expenses, is, by law, invested in Federal securities which earn interest for the social security trust funds.

It is truthful to say that *"under the law"*, the money collected as social security taxes can be used *only* to pay social security benefits and administration expenses. The law does say just that. (Sec. 401 U.S. Code, Subchapter II—Federal Old-Age, Survivors, & Disability Insurance Benefits). But it is false, misleading and untruthful to imply that what in fact happens is that a special reserve fund has actually been set aside with all the Social Security taxes out of which only social security benefits and administrative expenses are paid.

Section 401(a) of the U.S. Code says

> "There is created on the books of the Treasury of the United States a trust fund to be known as the 'Federal Old Age and Survivors Insurance Trust Fund'."

This "trust fund" is supposed to contain 100 percent of the social security taxes. Subd. (d) of Sec. 401 then goes on to say:

> It shall be the duty of the Managing Trustee to *invest* such portion of the Trust Funds as is not, in his judgment, required

to meet current withdrawals. Such investments may be made *only* in interest bearing obligations of the United States. . . .

Can you imagine the XYZ Insurance Company being allowed to "invest" its reserves by spending them all for executive salaries and entertainment expenses, and then substituting its own IOU as a "reserve" out of which it will hope to pay annuities or benefits to its policy-holders?

It is interesting to note that a subsequent 48 page booklet entitled "Your Social Security" was issued in October 1965 (OASI-35) which included "information about 'Medicare' and other recent changes in the Social Security Law." In place of the word "taxes" there was substituted the euphemism "contributions". In place of the word "trust" in describing the funds which were to provide the payments, there was substituted the word "special" on some occasions, and on still other occasions the clearly false, misleading and deceptive term "trust fund" is still retained.

In a later Social Security Administration booklet entitled "If You Become Disabled" (OASI-29 December 1965) the statement is again made on page 2

> The basic idea of social security is a simple one: During working years employees, their employers, and self-employed people pay social security contributions, which go into *special* funds; and when earnings stop or are reduced because the worker retires, dies, or becomes disabled, monthly cash benefits are paid *from the funds* to replace part of the earnings the family has lost.

In another Social Security Administration booklet entitled "Your Social Security Earinings Record" (OASI-93, July 1966) the question is posed on page 19:

"WHERE DOES THE MONEY COME FROM?"

The wholly false and misleading answer is supplied by the Government on page 21.

> "Under the law, the money in these trust funds can be used only to pay social security benefits and the costs of administering the retirement, survivors, disability, and health insurance programs.
>
> Money not immediately needed for benefit payments and administrative expenses is, by law, invested in Federal securities which earn interest for the trust funds.
>
> Contributions under the schedules shown on page 20, with interest earnings from the trust funds' investments, maintain the financial soundness of the retirement, survivors, and disability insurance and hospital insurance programs."

The "contributions" are purely and simply a device used to collect more income taxes to be used for anything. Labeling it "contributions" cannot disguise its true nature. It is another income tax with no deductions for dependents, etc., but with a constantly rising rate and a rising ceiling of earnings subject to the tax. The Government does not explain how it is able to earn interest on its own obligations.

Actually the Social Security System is founded on a devious scheme of directly taxing current production exactly as the correctly labeled income tax does. However under the guise of establishing a true pension plan for themselves, the workers are hoodwinked into offering virtually no resistance to the Social Security tax and they actually embrace with loving care the hand that stealthily reaches into their pockets. On the surface and spelled out in the law itself, the right to receive Social Security benefits is keyed to the individual's work record and amounts paid in by him or in his behalf. Actually however the payments themselves are financed practically entirely from current tax receipts.

Recognition of the Social Security System as a giant hoax in this respect is exemplified in the following discussion that took place in connection with the proposal leading to Medicare from the House Ways and Means Committee Executive Hearings on Medical Care for the Aged, 1st Session, 89th Congress (1965), Part 1, p. 20:

Mr. Byrnes, So that fundamentally what we are doing here is not prepaying, but what we are doing here is having the people who are currently working finance the benefits of those currently over 65?

Mr. Myers. I think it can be viewed that way, just as the old-age and survivors insurance trust fund can, or else you can also view that it is prepayment in advance on a collective group basis, so that the younger contributors are making their contributions with the expectation that they will receive the benefits in the future-and not necessarily with the thought that their money is being put aside and earmarked for them, but rather that later there will be current income to the system for their benefits.

Mr. Byrnes. In other words, on the theory that if I am going to be asked to pay for a tax today for a benefit that is available to people over 65, then when I get to be 65 somebody who is then working ought to do the same thing for me? Is that it?

Mr. Myers. Yes: I would say that is the way it is, and this is a reasonable group prepayment basis, I think you can call it, because of the compulsory nature of the tax for now and for all time to come on people in covered employment.

So we see that a worker does not pay in anything anywhere which is earmarked or set aside for his own account, not one red cent. When he reaches a pre-determined age, other workers are forced to pay him out of their wages, just as he himself did for others. Occasionally some Social Security official will admit to the truth. Witness the statement made in 1964 by the Chief Actuary of the Social Security Administration. "For those now on the rolls, it is likely that they would have paid, *at most*, for about 10 % of the benefits actually payable to them." Even if the 10% has been paid by a wage earner, no part of that was paid specifically for himself or set aside in his own behalf.

The so-called Social Security Trust Fund is merely a book-keeping entry. Tax collections of every kind in 1970 will be the source of the Social Security checks that go out in that year. The billions collected annually out of virtually every pay-roll in America, do not go into a separately ear-marked trust fund or special account. The misnamed "social security fund" contains only a fraction of one percent of the presently accrued liability. The social security payments deducted each week can be and are used to put a man on the moon, for general war and defense purposes, for paying farmers for not producing, for foreign aid, and the myriad ventures into which the State may decide to take a fling.

The concepts built up so assiduously since the inception of Social Security that the worker was getting a pension in exchange for and in proportion to his enforced savings recently has been overtly discarded. The government has now decided to send checks to everyone seventy-two or over even if he or she never contributed one penny to the Social Security System. As of November 1, 1966, Social Security pensions are being paid to that group, concededly out of general revenues and again regardless of the need of the recipient. The false concept of Social Security as insurance has been overtly discarded, first in Medicare and now with Social Security pensions going to non-contributors.

It should also be noted, in passing, that anyone eligible for social security payments, now forfeits all or a part of those payments, if he or she earns more than $1680.00 a year. This is another gimmick and points up the dishonesty of the Social Security System. The purchaser of an annuity from a private insurance company has his rights fixed and pre-determined by the insurance contract and at the end of the contract period gets what he bargained for, with no strings attached. If he contracted to get his annuity at age 65, he will get it then and he can decide for himself whether he wants to continue working or not, and will not be penalized if he decides to keep on working. After all he has earned his annuity in accordance with his contract and the insurance company must pay off and can get no windfall.

A great deal of the popularity of the Social Security System in America, rests upon the assumption that government sponsored social security is a form of old-age insurance, very much like annuities of life insurance policies with varying options, sold by private insurance companies. Most workers who pay social security taxes believe that they are putting away a savings fund for their old age and that any promised retirement benefits will simply be a part of their own savings coming back to them. The deal is sweetened, they feel, by the matching contribution of their employer plus the increment earned and added by the astute management of the "trust fund" by the government officials which further enhances the value of the combined tax.

They believe that the promise of a pension under the Social Security program is quite as secure and has as much value as the prospect of future income from personally owned and controlled private property, whether deposited in a savings bank at interest or otherwise invested. The experience of many of the early beneficiaries of the Social Security program leaves the distinct feeling that here is a far less costly thing than private insurance coverage and quite a bargain to boot, almost like something for nothing and guaranteed by the government beside.

Recent Social Security Administration literature continues the deception. In a 1968 brochure distributed by it by the carload entitled "Recent Improvements in Your Social Security" it says:

> The amended program, like the former program, is soundly financed. The income from contributions, plus the interest earnings of the Social Security trust funds, will be sufficient to pay all present and future benefits provided in the law and all the administrative expense of the program.

Now even if the Social Security boys in Washington are still deluded by the myth of a "trust fund" surely even they must know that there is no money in the till to pay "future benefits provided in the law."

Dr. Dean Russell a member of the staff of the Foundation for Economic Education wrote an article in *The Freeman* entitled "Why Social Security Must Fail", in which he said:

> When our government officials tell us that our social security funds are (like private insurance premiums) also invested and earn a return of three percent, you might laugh— or perhaps cry. For the so-called "social security fund" is strictly nominal, since it amounts to less than one per cent of today's liability. Even then, this woefully inadequate fund is "invested" by government in the government's own bonds. The interest that the government "earns" from its investment necessarily comes from you and me in the form of more taxes; there is no other place it can come from. That is why the government's social security scheme was mathematically and necessarily bankrupt from its inception; it was (and is) merely a political mechanism designed for persons who can be lulled

into believing that the police power of government is the proper moral and financial base on which to build a sound retirement program.

The harsh reality of our financially and morally unsound social security program must be faced sooner or later; if not by our generation, then by our children and grandchildren. True enough, increases in premiums (up to some unknown point) can probably postpone the eventual collapse and the revolution that may follow it. Increased inflation can also be used by government to prolong the life of that unsound scheme. But our social security program must collapse eventually, since it is founded on continuing and automatic losses for the participants as a group.

Another example of tricky and deceitful government journalese is contained in the one page flyer sent out over the signature of Robert M. Ball, Commissioner of Social Security, announcing payments to anyone over 72, rich or poor, who had never paid a cent into the Social Security System (Form SSA-L 171-7/66)

Instead of saying now you can get some cash merely by proving you reached 72, the government broadside announced "You may be entitled to a *benefit* of $35- a month under a new law." The one page sheet called the handout not cash or a check but either "benefit" or "special benefit" no less than eight times.

The basic idea is no longer basic. Whether they are called "special benefits" or "trust" or "special" funds, whether they are labelled "taxes" or "contributions" the veil has been pierced and the true nature of the scheme is clearly revealed to be hand-outs paid out of general tax collections, and the "trust funds" just as fast as they come in have been commingled and spent along with all other tax collections.

That this is so appears quite clearly from an analysis of an official interview reported in the U.S. News and World Report for December 7, 1964, in which Robert M. Ball, Commissioner of Social Security, was asked the following questions and gave the following answers:

Q Mr. Ball, are people's Social Security pensions safe?

A Oh, yes, I would say that they are absolutely and completely safe.

Q For persons who retire in the future, as well as for those already retired?

A Yes, for both groups.

People who are now getting pensions will continue to get them, and those who are entitled to pensions in the future will be able to draw them in the amounts the law contemplates.

Q What is the guarantee?

A It's this. The Social Security program has been set up in such a way that, taking the system as a whole, the contributions paid by workers and employers and the self-employed, plus the interest earned by the Social Security trust fund, will meet all benefit costs as they fall due in the future.

Now, it is true that there is a need for a small reallocation of income between the old-age and survivors part. But this can easily be handled, and without any increase in over-all contribution rates. Remember that Congress, from the beginning, has been very, very careful to provide for full financing whenever benefits have been increased. Costs of the program have been increased significantly, but the scheduled contribution rates have been increased to cover the costs.

Q What is the assurance that this kind of balance will be continued in the future?

A Mainly the strong determination of all concerned to see to it that the program is soundly financed. Congress has shown that it will take no chances on this.

As a safeguard, the financing of the program is studied and reported on regularly by a board of trustees and reviewed by an advisory council composed of people from outside the Government.

Nothing is left undone to keep the program sound.

Q You mentioned the Social Security Trust Fund. What is that?

A It is a fund that stands back of Social Security benefits and can be used only for this purpose. It is, first of all a contingency reserve for periods when outgo might be greater than income because, for example, of a decline in employment. Secondly, the funds earn interest and thus help to meet benefit costs.

Q How much is now in that reserve fund, or trust fund?

A About 22 billion dollars in the old-age and survivors insurance fund and the disability insurance fund combined.

Let us examine the honesty of the language used and the integrity and collateral behind the guarantee.

The Social Security "trust" fund is an ephemeral one. The official estimate of the size of the fund in 1969 was twenty-five billion, more than twenty-three billion of which was "invested" in United States Government securities. Instead of a true reserve fund, to guarantee its obligations, the Social Security "Trust fund" has a virtually empty cash register, just about enough to cover one month's checks and is really on a pay as you go basis for Old Age and Survivors insurance. But OASI had obligations totaling three hundred and forty five billion. This is a real guarantee and insurance that the Social Security System will never be eliminated because the government cannot go out and borrow the difference of some three hundred and twenty billion dollars to pay off these obligations. It will pay them off, of course, with dollars taken out of the pay envelopes of workers yet unborn and other tax dollars, which depreciated dollars will in all probability, be worth five or ten cents as the years roll on.

Further on in the interview, Mr. Ball was questioned about the "trust fund"

Q Getting back to the reserve fund: In what form does the fund hold that 22 billion dollars?

A In U.S. Government bonds.

Q The Government, in other words, has borrowed the money—

A Yes, and put up bonds for it.

Q So the money has been spent, and is not there in the fund at all—

A It is true, of course, that the Government—as a borrower from the fund, just as it would as a borrower from a bank— has used the cash. The fund, instead of holding cash, holds Government bonds, and earns a return on those bonds. The Government has an obligation to the trust fund, as it would have to an individual or bank or corporation it had borrowed from. That obligation is pay interest and repay the principal.

Q Some people find it hard to believe there really is a reserve fund. Is there a fund when the Government has already borrowed and spent the money?

A Of course there is a fund, and no less real than if the money were there in cash.

I'm always surprised at the persistence of the idea that the fund is gone. This has been answered authoritatively many, many times.

I think it's clear, on analysis, that the situation is this: If the Government did not borrow from the trust fund, it would have to borrow an equal amount from others—say, the banks or the general public. Then, when the time came to pay off the bonds and interest, the Government would have to collect taxes or else borrow to pay the banks or the general public.

It's exactly the same way with the Social Security funds. To the extent the Social Security trust funds—instead of other bond-holders—receive interest in the future, it is not necessary to get as much income from Social Security contributions. If there were no Social Security funds, general taxes or borrowing would have to be equally high to pay the private bondholders and, in addition, Social Security contributions would have to be higher to make up for the lack of interest income.

Q And the Government's commitment to the Social Security fund is the same as the commitment it has to any other holder of Government bonds?

A Exactly the same. To the same extent that the Government's credit is good, the Social Security fund is sound.

A greater collection of nonsense and double-talk would be hard to find. The Social Security Commissioner concedes, in just so many words, that the "trust fund" is a myth. The Government borrowed the money, spent it, and put up its I.O.U. in the Treasury to record the transaction.

By some legerdemain, the I.O.U. has now become an asset of the borrower. When a business man borrows money, he and his accountants as well as his creditors and his bankers know it is a debt. However, when the Government does the same thing, in some mysterious fashion it becomes an asset and becomes collateral for an obligation, or accounts payable. It is so ludicrous that only because of the use of the big lie technique by being propounded time and again, the point is reached that even the government liars themselves begin to believe it. When Commissioner Ball says he is surprised at the persistence of the idea that the trust fund is gone, he really shoudn't be. The reason that the idea that the fund has vanished persists, is due to the simple fact that it is true.

The clear proof that the bonds referred to are not an asset but a liability, is the fact that the government having tapped the till and spent all the money, now must pay interest on the I.O.U.'s (bonds) it substituted for the cash. Of course when the bond falls due, the debtor must pay off the principal or get the creditor's consent for an extension. The latter is what happens when the government issues new bonds and because of its power, not its inherent solvency, gets more time to pay. If the bonds were like the bonds insurance companies purchase both from government and private industry for their portfolio as a reserve for their obligations, the government would be receiving instead of paying interest. Can you imagine lending your money to someone and then paying him interest on the money he borrowed from you besides! If you can swallow that, then the whole hocus pocus of Social Security makes sense and you need not read on any further.

On the other hand, if your intelligence causes you to rebel at accepting that, then pursuing this inquiry to its conclusion might be worth the trouble, especially if you can tell the difference between an asset and a liability.

Alanson W. Willcox, a former counsel for the Social Security Board, has courageously come out for honest bookkeeping. In an article, originally unsigned, published in the *Quarterly Journal of Economics* in May 1937 he compares the so-called reserve of the Social Security System with the true reserves of a commercial insurance company. He asserts that the Social Security reserve is actually a statement of the liability of the federal government for future benefits, rather than a sum set aside from the excess of payroll taxes over disbursements.

To the same effect is this comment by T.H. Eliot, another former counsel for the Social Security Board:

> Honest bookkeeping seems to require that this increasing obligation be shown on the books of the United States.

The honest bookkeeping required to properly reflect the cost of the Great Society is still lacking. The books and ledgers are still crooked.

If I lose $1000 at the race track which I took out of my right side pants pocket, and then I put my own beautifully engraved bond bearing interest at 5% in my left side pants pocket, is this a good substitute for the lost $1000.?

If, on the other hand, on leaving the track I borrow $1000 from my friend John, who had a more successful day, and give him my I.O.U. or bond, the true picture of the day's events present itself. I am poorer by $1000 and John is richer to that extent, provided of course, my credit and my I.O.U. or bond is good, and I repay John.

The bonds in the Social Security "trust fund" are the same as my own I.O.U. in my pocket. No man is wealthier because he owes himself some money. The bonds or I.O.U.'s in the Social Security "trust fund" were issued by the United States Government (via the Treasury Department) and are also owned by and deposited with the United States Government (via the Social Security Administration). The respective bureaus are merely agents of the same principal and it is fraudulent for the Government to treat the bonds as an asset on the Social Security balance sheet.

In *1984* George Orwell prophetically pointed out how the managers of the news and our leaders distort the meaning of words. By their propaganda under the guise of education coupled with their power of the purse, and all the other means available exclusively to them, those running the show falsify our customary understanding of words to the point where to serve political ends they take on a completely new sense.

Brainwashing is a post-Orwellian term now in general use. Totalitarian states, with minor variations, are now called People's Democratic Republics. Can you imagine a country calling itself a fascist dictatorship? The very worst appellation will be Christian Democrat or some variable like Social Democrat. Russia is classified among peace-loving and freedom-loving powers thus qualifying for membership in the United Nations. Call yourself a liberal or progressive and you are equated "good"—Conservative is bad. In John Stuart Mill's time, the reverse was true. Remember that the three Party slogans promulgated by the Ministry of Truth in "1984" were:

WAR IS PEACE
FREEDOM IS SLAVERY
IGNORANCE IS STRENGTH.

V

• • • • • • • • •

Something For Nothing

IS there such a thing as a "free" lunch? Or is the free lunch concept typical of the "free" retirement money or "free" medical and hospital benefits or the other "free" services furnished by a benevolent State? In the old days of the free lunch which generally was available to saloon patrons at the end of or opposite the bar at which they were imbibing, the customers knew that they were paying for their lunch with their purchases of beer or whiskey. Unfortunately this same realization seems to be missing today and the myth persists that the free lunch in the form of government handouts is really and truly free and at no cost to anyone. This is the great illusion of our times.

One absolute which should be ever present in the minds of a skeptical alert citizenry is that the State produces nothing. When it gives you something, whether gratis or at some ostensibly bargain cost to you, remember that first it has taken this from you in hidden or direct taxes, and then gives you back only a part of what it took, the balance being retained for a handling charge.

The Welfare State is based on the theory that it gives its people something for nothing. I have never seen any propaganda which, upon analysis, suggests otherwise. If the people were told their government is taking their wealth, keeping some of it for political job-holding administrative purposes, and then redistributing it to them in "welfare" benefits, I daresay the welfare state would be short lived.

As the Government take increases, welfare programs proliferate, and the need for additional welfare grows. There never seems to be a point at which the welfare demands are satisfied but the illusion is ever-present that if only more money is thrown at the problem it will go away.

This same myth of something for nothing, got short shrift when green stamps or other "gifts" were widely distributed "free" to the house-wife with each purchase at the supermarket. Before long, she realized that the merchant who did not give out "free" green stamps, was able to and did undersell the one who did, and she switched her business accordingly. However, she apparently hasn't caught on to the same government hoax because there is no competition and no standard of comparison to expose that deception.

If the tax money taken from the individual were permitted to stay with him, he would buy his own "welfare", if he were so inclined, in the form of pensions, medical care, education, etc., which would be competitively priced. If the taxpayer preferred to spend a greater proportion of his income now for housing rather than for a pension or education, the choice should be his. After all, it is his hard earned money and the prerogative should be his.

This is not designed to to deny assistance to the unfortunate indigent and ill aged or the physically or mentally handicapped, but to channel help where there is a genuine need for it and not diffused in insignificant amounts where it will do little or no good. As society or a community becomes more affluent, the need for welfare should diminish but the opposite seems to be the rule.

A glaring example of what happens when a democratic welfare state continues to vote more and more "free" benefits for its citizens is Uruguay. That nation gave away so many "free" welfare benefits, among them full retirement pay at 55 years of age, that it went broke. Inflation ran rampant, as high as 85% in one year, and to its sorrow, it has learned that passing a law doesn't produce more wealth and you can't distribute what you first don't produce. They learned the hard way that man still lives by the sweat of his brow.

The United States doesn't seem to learn by example. We are being indoctrinated with the philosophy that without Social Security people would go hungry and starve and that all Americans are in need of a handout of some kind. Expansive welfare programs both as to amount and kind are the order of the day. In ancient Greece they used to say that whom the Gods would destroy they first made mad. Currently this can be paraphrased by saying making them slaves of the State precedes their destruction.

Social Security has become a sacred cow, and is the current prominent example of Government promises of a "free" lunch on the house for everyone. At election time, politicians vie with each other in promising expanded benefits. Many pollsters doomed Barry Goldwater as soon as he deigned to criticize Social Security, particularly after a campaign speech in the New Hampshire primary in 1964 when he said that perhaps compulsory Social Security should be abolished and made voluntary. After all, twenty five million voters presently receiving monthly social security checks at a monthly rate of more than $2 billion (to say nothing of their relatives, friends, and those about to retire) are not to be sneezed at.

Being a politician, after his defeat in the New Hampshire primary, Goldwater recanted and thereafter said he was misunderstood. What he really wanted, he emphasized, was to strengthen the Social Security System. But it was too late to try to explain his use of that dreadful word "voluntary" when he stated on the first day of his campaign in the New Hampshire primary, "I think Social Security should be made voluntary. This is the only definite position I have on it. If a man wants it, fine. If he doesn't want it, he can provide his own." Rockefeller quickly exploited Goldwater's faux pas asserting that a voluntary Social Security System would bankrupt it. It was hopelessly insolvent anyway, as we have seen since virtually the entire Social Security "reserve" fund was only in Government I.O.U.'s.

In an article in the *Washington Post*, John Chamberlain wrote:

> The original Goldwater statement on [voluntary] Social Security followed the publication of a poll taken in Britain, which indicated that more than 50 percent of the English voters would like to have the opportunity to contract out of Government welfare schemes. "Contracting out" implies that welfare must be kept up, but that a choice would be allowed between the public and private kinds.

The thought logically presents itself that if the Social Security System as administered in America is so actuarily sound and so much more attractive than a private old-age pension plan, why should this dire fear persist that the consequences of permitting a choice would be catastrophic.

Politicians are not alone in their adoration of Social Security. We don't expect too much from them when it comes to making sense in matters involving economics and it may be due to the fact that they have learned the little they know from professors of the dismal science in our institutions of higher learning. Witness, for example, the twaddle from the pen of the great Professor Paul A. Samuelson of M.I.T. in the *Newsweek* of February 3, 1967, and I quote:

PAUL A. SAMUELSON
On Social Security

Which program of the modern welfare state has been, by all odds, most successful? Undoubtedly, the social-security program. And it is a remarkable fact that both expert and layman will agree on this judgment. . . .

SOMETHING FOR NOTHING?

Social insurance makes sense because we are all in the same boat. All of us are going to die; most of us face a period of retirement before death. It is a good way to run a railroad to take account of this basic symmetry.

The beauty about social insurance is that it is *actuarially unsound.* Everyone who reaches retirement age is given benefit privileges that far exceed anything he has paid in. And exceed his payments by more than ten times as much (or five times, counting in employer payments)!

How is this possible? It stems from the fact that the national product is growing at compound interest and can be expected to do so for as far ahead as the eye cannot see. Always there are more youths than old folks in a growing population. More important, with real incomes growing at some 3 per cent per year, the taxable base upon which benefits rest in any period are much greater than the taxes paid historically by the generation now retired. And social security, unlike actuarially funded insurance, is untouched by inflation: after Germany's terrible 1923 inflation, private insurance was wiped out but social insurance started all over as if nothing had happened.

Social security is squarely based on what has been called the eighth wonder of the world—compound interest. A growing nation is the greatest Ponzi game ever contrived. And that is a fact, not a paradox.

Now I submit that if Social Security is the eighth wonder of the world, the good professor is the ninth if he can sell this something for nothing philosophy to the American public. What Professor Samuelson likes about Social Security is that it is "actuarily unsound". But the Government in all its literature proclaims endlessly that it is actuarily sound. Somebody is lying or stupid. In a pamphlet issued by the Social Security Administration (OASI-36, October 1966) entitled "Financing YOUR SOCIAL SECURITY BENEFITS" right in the beginning, it says

> The social security program as a whole is soundly financed, its funds are properly invested, and on the basis of actuarial estimates that the Council has reviewed and found sound and appropriate, provision has been made to meet all of the costs of the program both in the short run and over the long-range future.
>
> Report of the Advisory Council on
> Social Security, January 1, 1965"

In a later pamphlet "Recent Improvements in YOUR SOCIAL SECURITY 1967 SOCIAL SECURITY AMENDMENTS" (SS1-1967-1 January 1968)" it says

> The amended program, like the former program, is soundly financed. The income from contributions, plus the interest earnings of the social security trust funds, will be sufficient to pay all present and future benefits provided in the law and all the administrative expenses of the program. The income to the program is estimated to exceed benefit and administrative costs for every year over the long-range future.

The truth is, of course, as is conclusively shown in Chapter IX that the younger workers are getting a raw deal and like all Ponzi schemes, Social Security does not and cannot make all of us rich, and actuarily speaking, it is a joke.

The Federal budget is a paradigm of the free lunch philosophy. In it we find something "free" for almost everybody from which we can only conclude that all of us in varying degrees must of necessity get some assistance from Washington. How we ever managed to survive without Social Security must remain an enigma for historians to ponder.

At the present time, it is estimated that we are forced to pay about forty percent of our income to local, state and Federal Governments in a variety of taxes. The rate of this take and the amount thereof have been growing at an alarming rate particularly considering that we are formally not at war.

Embodied in the welfare statist program of President Johnson, Congress enacted a far reaching and sweeping expansion of Social Security. He has said, "this Nation of abundance can surely afford . . . to assure all citizens of decent living standards regardless of economic reverses or the vicissitudes of human life and health."

From 1966 on the monthly payments in addition to existing ones to cover the continuing expansion of benefits will amount to another one and a half billion dollars plus still another billion projected for the payment of hospital bills for those over 65, again whether they are in need or not.

Sotto voce comes a boost in Social Securtiy taxes from both employee and employer. President Johnson, signing Medicare into law, spoke of a deduction of only a "small amount each payday." But why complain? Are you for sickness and against good health? Are you against old people? Or against widows and orphans?

The implications of this hand-out, co-incidentally in an election year, are clear. In the future, as in all government schemes of this nature, we "ain't seen nothin yet". This prediction is already coming true.

President Johnson in a speech in San Antonio, Texas, on April 8, 1966, said: [*New York Times*—4/9/66]

> I would like to improve insurance protection for the widows and the orphans. I would like to keep our Social Security and public welfare programs up to date in relation to increased earnings.
>
> I would like for our individuals now on welfare rolls to be provided additional incentives for them to find work.
>
> And Medicare need not just be for people over 65. That is where we started.
>
> I have been wondering for some time now why we shouldn't bring our compassion and our concern to bear not just on people over 65 but upon our young children under 6.
>
> . . . I want to let you in on another secret: That is one of the reasons I asked John Gardner, because of my concern for these young folks, to create new plans for a new program that you haven't ever heard before, to assist in financing dental services for children.
>
> Luci spent all the way down here this morning fussing at me because I didn't say eye services for children.
>
> We are going to have these new plans and we are going to have these new programs.

The cat was now out of the bag. Parents are no longer necessary. Turn the babies over to the great white father and stop worrying about them.

What of the present and future administrations? We can be sure that the politicians of both major parties, including Mr Nixon, will try to out-do each other while making their promises of greater pies in the sky. The price tag goes up with each election campaign and in general, as we have seen, the promises are fulfilled, contrary to what usually happens to pre-election promises. Social Security has too great an impact on the Social Security beneficiaries to be treated in a cavalier fashion and that voting bloc does not forget.

"Because some Social Security recipients have been getting benefits 10 times as great as what they have paid in, people seem to think we have a special machine here which turns out $10 bills for $1 bills," says a top official of the Social Security Administration. [*Barron's National Business Weekly*—4/26/65]

Well, isn't this something devoutly to be desired? This is the bonanza that a great number of the beneficiaries have already received. As for those entering the system now or within recent years, they will carry a crushing burden in making current payments. The deductions now being taken out of the worker's pay envelope will in no way made up for the pension he will receive. However, now the pitch is that while after a thorough examination Social Security may prove to be not such a good thing for the new worker, it is "for the social good". In any event, it is well meant so bless it and don't be too critical of it.

The paradox of want in the midst of wealth still persists. The solution which promises to conquer poverty in our time is basically the Social Security System, so we are told to be patient and to have faith in our leaders who will lead us unto the promised land of the great society.

There is only one possible way under Social Security that the Government can provide old-age pensions for retired workers. Those who still work must furnish the wherewithal to pay the pensions as they fall due. We live on current production and if there were a universal work stoppage it would be only a matter of days or at the most weeks before we would all starve.

In the first twenty years of Social Security, the Government collected 25 billion in Social Security taxes which it promptly spent on everything but pensions for the retired. Subsequently it taxed the same workers and their employers again to pay the promised benefits. It would be difficult to conceive of a more dishonest and fake "insurance" scheme.

The truth is that the promise of a social security pension will be fulfilled only because of the taxing power of the government. This is its only asset as distinguished from the real assets of a private insurance company which might make the same contractual promise with its policy holder. The fact that the government issues bonds only serves to conceal the truth. Even if there were no bonds or I.O.U.'s issued, no government in power would default on the promise and the Social Security payments would be made when due. The bonds only serve to compound the crime since they are used as an inflationary device to facilitate the pay-off in depreciated currency. In this connection the question is sometimes raised as to how much the Federal Government really owes. The statutory national debt as of this writing is over $360 billion. This debt ceiling does not cover the government's contingent liabilities, which have been increasing at a rate greater than the increase in the statutory debt ceiling. It has been estimated that these liabilities could push the figure up to over a trillion dollars. The Social Security System itself has obligations totaling over $350 billion and for this reason alone the Social Security System can never be cancelled or eliminated, disregarding the political holocaust that would descend on any administration that had the temerity even to suggest it. The Government cannot go out in the search for funds and borrow the billions required to pay off the Social Security obligations nor can it repudiate them any more than it can directly renege on any of its other obligations. What it certainly will do, as it has in the past, and what it can only do in the future, is pay off with cheaper dollars.

When Congress votes for an expanded Social Security program, as it does from time to time, particularly near election, it is aware of the fact that there is no such thing as a free lunch or free retirement or free Medicare. Even the government acutaries have acknowledged that a new entrant into the Social Security System is scheduled to pay $1.69 in social security taxes for every $1.00 promised him in benefits. The spread will become wider with the enlarged base subject to Social Security taxes and the increase in rates. As I will establish in Chapter IX, a young person would get a much better deal buying his security in the form of an annuity from a private insurance company instead of buying government promised security in the form of a Social Security pension.

The inadequacy of Social Security as a hedge against the economic hazards of modern day life is evidenced by the fact that United States insurance companies now have over one trillion dollars worth of life insurance in force backed up by real assets. They will pay off even if they do not sell another policy. In 1966 the American public despite increased Social Security benefits made record purchases of $121 billion worth of life insurance. This is twice what it bought ten years ago and indicates the lack of security afforded by expansive dollar amounts of Social Security benefits.

In general people realize there is no "free lunch". They bought hospital care in the form of Blue Cross Plans and Americans also used their own money to assure their ability to pay their doctors through Blue Shield Plans, about 53 million persons being enrolled in Blue Shield as of the end of 1965. Social Security Bulletin for February 1969 reports:

> *Private Health Insurance* in 1967 continued its expansion in terms of number of people covered, premiums and benefit expenditures, and proportion of consumer health expenditures met by insurance benefits. Between 75 percent and 87 percent of the civilian population under age 65 (depending on the source of data) had some health insurance coverage of hospital expense at the end of 1967 and between 73 percent and 80 percent had some coverage of surgical expense. The proportion of the population under age 65 with some coverage of physician visits in the hospital was about 66 percent.

It was further reported that a substantial number of persons aged 65 and over have private health insurance coverage complementary to Medicare. Approximately 50 percent of the aged have some private health insurance coverage of hospital care, and about 40 percent have some coverage of surgical expense. It is apparent that our streets would not be clogged with the sick and the dying, even without Medicare and Social Security. In addition prices for hospital and medical services would not have reached these exhorbitant levels without the inflationary push created by the Government.

In the Social Security scheme the worker is led to believe he is getting a better deal than he could purchase for himself because his boss also is required to contribute equally to the mythical trust fund which will ultimately be used for his sole benefit. With regard to unemployment insurance, Medicare, and pensions for government workers, in addition to the worker and his employer, the politician asserts that the Government makes a contribution also in varying percentages. However, on analysis this proves to be a lot of nonsense.

What it all boils down to is that the worker picks up the entire tab which in theory was to be split three ways. His own share like Social Security deductions and income tax withholding comes right out of his pay envelope before he even gets to see it. He also pays his employer's share since it is reflected in the enhanced price of everything produced by human labor which is everything he buys. In addition he pays the so-called government share in the multitude of other taxes and levies because having no money of its own, there really is no other way the Government can put up its share.

The thrifty who worked, planned, and saved for their own retirement as well as those who counted on their Social Security pensions to take care of their basic needs, have seen their retirement benefits wiped out by inflation, caused largely by the very Government that presumed to help them. For example average weekly earnings of non-agricultural workers increased by $7.65 or nearly 8% between January 1966 and December 1967. But for a man with three dependents, spendable income-take home pay in constant prices-declined during this period. For those with fixed incomes, the effects were more obvious—a loss in real income of about 6.1%. And the trend has continued and accelerated.

An observable side effect is that the man who expects that his Social Security tax will be a hedge against his old age, and sees that hope shattered, will most likely lose whatever respect he had for frugality and thrift. When that happens the people will be content to put their snouts into and feed at the public trough and before long achieve the status of cattle. Some heads may roll while the drama unfolds but the politician hopes that the day of reckoning will not come while he is in office. His pragmatic philosophy is, "Get mine, promise the moon, live it up, and don't be concerned with what will happen in the long run. Perhaps I'll be dead by then, or hopefully at least out of office and my successor will be left holding the bag." As Keynes used to say "In the long run we are all dead."

The way it looks from here, the politician is correct. Before his chickens will have come home to roost, World War III will surely break out, the State will take over completely and past idiocies and promises will be obliterated and forgotten in the struggle for survival.

It should be recalled that Herbert Hoover is identified with the great depression which began in 1929 and not his predecessors in office.

"*Aprés moi le deluge.*"

VI

• • • • • • • • •

Money, Political Power, and Expansion of the Welfare State

In the not too distant past, the American theory of government dictated that it should do only those things and provide only those services that the people could not do or provide for themselves. This political philosophy seems completely antiquated now and if any advocates of it can be found, they are promptly labelled reactionaries.

Our Founding Fathers and their political heirs right up to World War II would be shocked if they could see the goodies that Washington has now provided for its flock from the cradle to the grave. The cost of government in the United States in 1969 at the Federal, State, and local levels was $9,000.00 per second, twice the cost of 10 years ago, and still rising rapidly. Since 1955 the cost of new welfare activities has accounted for about 50% of the increase in Government spending, aside from defense items. Typical of this concern of the State is seen in the press releases and speeches that followed the adoption of one of the more exciting of the myriad welfare adventures of the Great Society.

"Medicare need not just be for people over 65." (*New York*

Times 4/9/66) President Johnson made this comment in expressing his hoped for expansion of the "Great Society", part of which plan he indicated was to include free dental services for children under six.

Since retirement is possible at 62, logically why shouldn't pensioners be entitled to get Medicare then too? Also if Medicare is available to all the people over 65 regardless of need, by what logic should it be denied to those of 60, or 50, or any age? Is the government so heartless and cruel that it will turn a deaf ear to the cries of a poor sick man who is only 64?

In the Welfare State, since the great white father is going to care for all of us, why shouldn't he care for us from the cradle to the grave? Why should there be any waiting period at all starting right from the time of birth or conception in the showering of his love and affection upon all his children?

The trend in that direction is clear as can be seen from the following statement made by Anthony J. Celebrezze, then Secretary of Health, Education, and Welfare commemorating the 30th Anniversary of the Social Security Act:

> "Our social security program assures a continuing income to millions of people too old or too young to support themselves by their own labor, or too sick to be able to work. In 30 years, this program has become an accepted part of our society. It responds to changes in need, population, technology, and the public interest." (Social Security Bulletin August 1965)

What he should have added was that without doubt the Social Security program will also inevitably respond to political needs and pressures.

Throughout the discussion of expanding benefits under Social Security, hardly ever is the cost mentioned. Rarely does a politician inveigh against the proposed increased benefit by relating it to the cost of paying for it. Perhaps the politicians hope that by ignoring the cost it will go away. In any event, no one will bring up the subject.

Not too long ago, when Senator Ribicoff was Secretary of Health, Education and Welfare, he expressed his opinion that a combined Social Security levy of not more than ten percent of payrolls was the practical maximum that could be obtained in addition to all the other levies, direct and indirect, on the wage earner. However, the increases scheduled by Congress already exceed this and will be over eleven percent by 1973, if not further increased in the meantime. If history is any indication of things to come, further increases are surely in the cards. A base of $15,000.00 has already been proposed.

Overall increases of 13% were the result of the Social Security Amendments of 1967 which provided augmented benefits for everyone receiving Social Security checks beginning with payments due in March, 1968, significantly or coincidentally, if you like, in an election year.

In a leaflet distributed in March 1968 by the Social Security Administration entitled "Your improved Social Security," all the increased Social Security benefits were detailed. Not one word was mentioned about where the money was coming from, not even a tiny suggestion about the source of the cornucopia. After all, why look a gift horse in the mouth? Hand out the largesse now and let tomorrow take care of itself.

If recent history tells us anything, new Welfare programs will proliferate, none will ever be terminated or phased out with its purposes accomplished, payrolls and bureaus will of necessity expand to administer them and taxes will inevitably be increased to finance them. When, as, and if the Viet Nam war ends, the fourteen cents out of every tax dollar now spent by the Government there will not be returned to the taxpayer in the form of reduced taxes but will be expended in new Welfare activities to meet the income made available. Any hopes to the contrary were clearly shattered by President Nixon when he addressed the National Governors Conference in Colorado Springs on Labor Day, 1969. President Nixon, too, had no more intention of letting the worker and capitalist enjoy the fruits of their increased production than his predecessors. In that speech he said "An effective strategy for peace makes possible an effective strategy for meeting our domestic needs".

In defining "our domestic needs" nothing was said by President Nixon about the urgent need of a general tax reduction for the overburdened taxpayer. What he did have to say was more of the same old tired clichés about reforming welfare, food programs for the needy, and a declaration that the "first five years of a child's life be a period of specific Federal concern," etc. The President said in his address that "dreams of unlimited billions of dollars being released once the war in Vietnam ends are just that—dreams. True, there will be additional money—but the claims on it already are enormous." One dream that will certainly be ignored is the plea of the writer for a reduction in his tax bill—his impossible dream.

The relation of money to private power is well known. The power of the state likewise is proportionate to its ability to get its citizens to "contribute" to it as much of their wealth or production as possible. If the people can be fooled into believing that direct taxes are all that is taken from them for the support of the monarch, the Lord of the Manor, Parliament, Congress, etc. so much the better. Social Security is one of the major methods of accomplishing precisely this deception for the bureaucracy in America thus serving to conceal the coercive nature of the State.

To put it bluntly, as of May 1970, there were more than 25 million monthly beneficiaries on Social Security. With their relatives they represent a voting bloc of well over 80 million votes. Due to the advancement of the medical science of geriatrics, more and more elderly people are direct recipients of monthly government checks and with Medicare and Medicaid the number of beneficiaries is constantly being increased. This tremendous voting power is fawned upon and catered to by the politicians in the most nauseating though deceptive fashion.

The propagation of the idea of accumulating an enormous reserve fund, just as private insurance companies do when they contract to pay annuities, was one step in the fraudulent scheme perpetrated by the government planners. The plan was promoted by the calculated deceit of using the words "insurance", "reserves," "security" etc. As a matter of fact, it was purely and simply another way of extracting taxes under the guise of a quid pro quo.Theoretically the social security "contributions" were to be used or exchanged for an actuarily sound funded pension plan. Nothing could be further from the truth. The many billions so collected were used for everything but building or investing in income producing properties calculated to provide pensions.

If the government got into a declared war or an undeclared police action anywhere in the world, Social Security taxes helped defray the cost. If the farmers were paid for taking part of their land out of production or to support the price of butter or peanuts or tobacco, Social Security taxes were used. You name it, the chances are Social Security funds paid for it.

The Santa Claus and Robin Hood philosophy of big government has been spelled out in detail in the recently published book *Encyclopedia of United States Government Benefits*. (Wm. H. Wise & Co. $9.95) It contains over one thousand pages and lists over ten thousand benefits that Big Daddy will supply to his children, from their cradle to their grave. An advertisement for the book says "YOUR CHILD'S EDUCATION-YOUR BUSINESS EXPANSION-YOUR VACATION HOME-YOU NAME IT." In extolling the virtues of the book and appealing to the cupidity in all of us, it continues ". . . plant trees on your property at no expense to you . . . travel in the United States and abroad at government expense. . . ."

There are other benefits closely related to but not directly embraced in Medicare and Social Security. One of these is called "Meals on Wheels". It was originated by the Office of Aging in the Department of Health Education and Welfare. Now elderly people can get a hot meal supplied by the government if they have no one to assist them in marketing for themselves. Washington will also give financial asistance to the rural landowner to facilitate the installation of riding stables, tennis courts, and golf courses. To prove that it is interested in the arts as well as sports, it has made a $20,000 grant for *A Biographical Dictionary and Census of Theatrical Performers on the Stages of London and its Suburbs from 1660 to 1801*. There is something for everyone—and all "free".

We should pause and recall the definition of the State over one hundred years ago by that wise French economic journalist Frederic Bastiat:

> "The great fictitious entity by which everyone seeks to live at the expense of everyone else."

Bastiat recognized, way back before the New Deal and the Great Society, that everyone would like a free ride and would not object to profiting from the labor of others. The vehicle to accomplish this would be the State as a respectable way of gratifying this desire. The only other way would be robbery. Bastiat commented:

"The state quickly understands the use it can make of the role the public entrusts to it. It will be the arbiter, the master, of all destinies. It will take a great deal; hence a great deal will remain for itself. It will multiply the number of its agents; it will enlarge the scope of its prerogatives; it will end by acquiring overwhelming proportions.

The current vehicle for "acquiring overwhelming proportions" is the Social Security System and the whole Great Society Syndrome.

When the State employs the methods Robin Hood used by taking from the "bad guys" (the haves) at the point of an arrow, and giving to the "good guys" (the have-nots), it is no longer guaranteeing security to society in general or to the "good guys" in particular. On the contrary it has become a destroyer of security by eliminating the incentive of the "haves" to produce more and to save. It has achieved the egalitarian effect of reducing the differential between the wealthy and the poor, and nothing else.

After the Social Security collections have been spent by the State on everything but Social Security, then as pension payments are required to be made, current Social Security taxes on employees and employers are used to pay off, and when these are inadequate as they now are, general tax revenues are then used to make up the deficit. The inevitable inflation accompanies the pay-off which can only be made with cheaper and cheaper dollars as is so apparent now.

In the meantime, the politicians have a constantly increasing sum of money to play with. As Bastiat predicted, their fertile minds are ever alert in devising schemes to justify their spending of the money instead of letting those who have earned it have the opportunity and pleasure of disposing of it themselves. The producers of the wealth may be smart enough in devising methods of becoming more efficient producers, but they are not qualified to spend the fruits of their labor. The non-producers assert that they are much better qualified as spenders of the other fellows' money and if there is any disagreement on that score it will do the producers no good to question their competence. Pay your taxes or go to jail. Papa knows best how to spend your pay. When election time comes around, then an appeal is made to the wisdom of the voter to put Mr. X in the White House rather than Mr. Y. The suggestion is usually made that the voter should ponder well the arguments put forth during the public debate, and upon mature deliberate consideration he will decide that Mr. X and his party and platform will prove best for the voter and the welfare of the country.

By a curious paradox, however, the wisdom of the voter stops after election day and does not extend to his freedom to decide how to provide for himself. He is a fool, and must therefore turn over a goodly portion of his income to a stranger who will know what is best for him and how to spend it for him.

Every local government, every city, county and state is enmeshed in the tentacles of the central government principally because of this enormous fund that it has to spend. If you have the connections and your local project is short of funds, provided you have voted right, go to Washington and some bureau will pick up the tab. Your gratitude will be expected when the votes are to be counted. Don't bite the hand that feeds you—remember that Washington gives out the fat contracts, so the business community also does not antagonize its best customer.

Unfortunately, too few of the voters look into the question of how the public purse got so fat. The power of big government today lies in its ability to give and give. It is its Santa Claus role of the great giver and not the great taker,that is embodied in the noble idea of the Welfare State. The people expect to receive more than they give. While this delightful expectancy can only be achieved by taking from some, a la Robin Hood, and giving to others, it is obviously impossible of being accomplished for all of us. Politicians are not famous for their forthrightness. At least the Socialists and Communists are honest when they advocate confiscation and a planned economy, operated by a powerful oligarchy. Americans do not realize that their government starts off with nothing, and can only give them at best what it first takes from them, minus a good fat handling or service charge.

With the fat purse at its disposal, this handling or service charge is first used to enhance the prestige and power of the political arm. Public relations men, news managers and speech writers abound in all bureaus to tell the voters how important are the bureaucratic tasks and how well they are being performed by the incumbents. It has been wisely said that the first task of an elected official is to lay the plans for his re-election. The more largesse he has to distribute, the more likely is he to be put back into office by the distributees.

During the Roosevelt New Deal era, Harry Hopkins succinctly characterized the methodology necessary to guarantee success at the polls. The formula was "tax and tax, spend and spend, elect and elect." In the intervening years, only the name of the game has been changed.

A staggering example of how some of the idiotic schemes of big government in applying this success formula affects us all was reported in the monthly economic letter of the First National City Bank of New York for May 1962.

It was there reported that President Kennedy had submitted to Congress a new program calling for tighter production controls to deal with the farm problem. While on the other hand, periodically the government launches investigations into the rising cost of living, it continues to spend billions of dollars to curtail production and support agricultural prices with the inevitably clear-cut effect of causing the very condition that alarms it. Between 1961 and 1968 the United States Government paid farmers 12 billion dollars for not producing wheat and feed grains alone. Of course, the investigations never result in faulting the government.

For the fiscal year ending June 30, 1962, the bank letter reported that total expenditures under the heading of Agriculture & Agricultural Resources are figured in the Federal budget for six billion three hundred forty three million dollars. Ponder well the following observation. Without this cost which was equivalent to $1700.00 for every farmer in America—it would not have been necessary to have any personal income tax rates exceeding twenty percent!

Another more current example of into what areas the government's fat purse will lead it on the way to being emptied is reported in the *New York Times* of September 4, 1966. In April of that year Sargent Shriver, the late president John F. Kennedy's brother-in-law, announced a Federal anti-poverty grant of $240,000.00 to create an experimental legal aid program in Wisconsin. To rhyme with "Medicare" this experiment was called "Judicare" and was under the aegis of the Office of Economic Opportunity. It is similar in operation to Medicare, and permits Judicare card holders to consult private lawyers, who charge $16.00 an hour which Judicare pays. The *Times* reports:

> This week, after six weeks of operation, Judicare was found to resemble a battle between the sexes more than a war on poverty. Virtually ignoring the loansharks, slumlords and business cheats who are supposed to be the oppressors of the poor, Judicare's clients were instead suing each other in divorce courts at a furious rate.
>
> Statistics released by the Judicare office here revealed that 84 percent of its cases so far have involved divorces. Of the first 86 cases, 63 were divorce suits and 9 were custody and support actions growing out of earlier divorces.

The Office of Economic Opportunity has already asked Congress for such legal aid next year to expand its program into other cities and states.

Under the anti-poverty legal aid program for Illinois, the town of Eldorado, population 3,573 is allotted $59,589. There are four lawyers there. In Karnak, Illinois, population 667, there has been set aside $65,805 for legal aid to the poor despite the fact that there are no lawyers there. Perhaps one will move from Eldorado.

There seems to be no end of such projects and others yet to come, which would have been inconceivable until recent times. No matter if on religious grounds alone the taxpayer might object to the government's financing divorces, he is not consulted. His Social Security taxes in the "trust fund" will pay to finance divorces and other crack-pot schemes the great brains in Washington may devise.

Big Government will get bigger in direct proportion to the size of its purse. As it gets its hands on more money, it surely will find or create projects on which to spend the extra green stuff. Inevitably, publicists and public relations men will laud the Administration then in power and justify the expenditures and perpetuate their own jobs.

It has been said that "If the Government did not do so much to hurt the people, it would not have to do so much to help them." Professor R.E. Slitor of the Economics Department at the University of Massachusetts has stated what looks like a corollary of Professor Parkinson's Law (Work expands so as to fill the time available for its completion) He noted: "Expenditure programs, as anyone with experience with family, club, PTA, or Governmental budget knows, will adequately assert themselves up to and beyond the available income."

The most effective way of stopping the State from hurting and then helping us is to sharply reduce the size of its bankroll. If we kept it poor, it would have to stay within the bounds prescribed by the legitimate exercise of Government activity and thousand page encyclopedias detailing Government benefits would become obsolete.

We have heard sometimes the facetious remark made by an unhappy taxpayer that the government should take his entire pay envelope intact and just pay his rent, food and other necessities of life out of it. Is it really so funny, or are we rapidly approaching that stage?

With the advance in geriatric care of our elderly, the voting power of this bloc will be staggering. The propensity of our politicians for pandering for these votes is an acknowledged fact of life. Remember the Townsend plan which advocated a uniform pension of $200.00 per month for everyone who attained the ripe old age of 60, the financing to be accomplished by a 2 percent transactions tax? Unfortunately, those who have attempted to provide for their old age themselves by being thrifty and conserving part of their earnings during their productive years, will be the primary sufferers by virtue of the fraud and deceit practiced upon them by the proponents of the Welfare State. This cruel deception is accomplished by that much misunderstood word "inflation", easily recognized in the continuously upward spiralling of wages and prices.

Wilbur Cohen, formerly Secretary of Health, Education and Welfare, has been influential in writing most of the social security laws since the inception of the Social Security Act. Senator Paul Douglas said in discussing him that "a Social Security expert is a man with Wilbur Cohen's telephone number." (*New Yorker Magazine*, 7/9/66, p. 70) He was candid enough recently to acknowledge the great political benefits that would accrue to those politicians who could sew up the voting power of our senior citizens by saying:

> When the Eisenhower people took over in 1953, they didn't seem to realize the immense political potential of this group. At the time, there were between twelve and thirteen million people over 65, and every day there were a thousand more, almost all of whom were eligible to vote, and most of whom did. That's a massive political bloc. Generally speaking, older people are conservatives, but not when it comes to Social Security increases or government participation in health care. (*New Yorker Magazine*, 7/9/66, p. 33)

The something for nothing philosophy, the free lunch syndrome, is ever present, and if by pandering to this numerically powerful group his election is insured, what politician would have the guts to tell the truth? In addition to the votes of the elderly, of course, there must be added the votes of the jobholders and their families who administer the vast Social Security program.

Myer Feldman, a man of some stature on President Kennedy's staff while he was in the White House and also in the Senate, said in discussing a proposed program to increase benefits for the aged:

> Sorenson and I worked long and hard on this entire problem throughout 1958. Wilbur Cohen frequently flew in from Michigan so that we could discuss things in detail, and he and I spent many hours, many nights, trying to set up a realistic program. Senator Kennedy was interested in the subject because of the growing number of older people in the population. He felt that Eisenhower had ignored many grave social problems, and that this was one of the gravest. Anyway, we discussed it off and on most of that year, mainly in terms of its social and political impact. We knew it was a big issue and getting bigger every month, and we felt that it could have a very great effect on the outcome of the Presidential election in 1960. (*New Yorker*, 7/9/66, p. 55)

From the foregoing it would seem that the callousness and insincerity of the politicians would be readily apparent to those who are appealed to for their votes. If the concern of the voter, whether senior or junior citizen, for the over-all welfare of his country, is subordinated to the "what's in it for me" approach, then the politician may get away with it for a while. When time proves, as it always has, that there is no free lunch, the current breed of rascals will be thrown out.

Since 1900, the life span of the average American has increased by more than twenty years, and all without a government administered medicare program. Private drug companies, in a profit oriented society, with tremendous funds allocated for research, and private foundations and charities, are largely responsible for this great advance.

I think it can be fairly said, that any one in America genuinely in need of medical attention, got it, and still gets it, whether he has providentially arranged for it at his own cost, or through private insurance, or is supplied it gratis at public expense.

In 1958, during hearings on the Forand bill to provide medical care for Social Security beneficiaries, the first witness for the Eisenhower administration, which opposed the legislation, was Marion B. Folsom, Secretary of Health, Education, and Welfare. He testified that between 1952 and 1958, the number of people covered by private hospitalization policies had increased from ninety-one million to one hundred and twenty million; those covered by surgical insurance policies rose from seventy-three million to one hundred and nine million; and those covered by general medical insurance policies doubled from thirty-six million to seventy-two million. Because of these tremendous increases in the private citizen's concern and provision for his own welfare, it was the administration's stand that this was the trend that should be encouraged, and that the government should stay out of that field. (*New Yorker*, 7/9/66, p. 41)

Despite the great increase in private protection plans since that time, the government has in effect pre-empted the field. This was accomplished not by offering a competitive voluntary insurance program to cover the hazards of unemployment caused by accident or ill health, or a better retirement program at a lesser cost than could be bought from a private insurance company, but by a compulsory program which must be paid for from taxes, and at a much greater cost. The consumer has no choice, any more than he may choose not to pay his income taxes, because he may disapprove of the way the government spends his hard earned money. His only alternative is to pay for the government plan and if he doesn't like it or it is inadequate, pay again for what he wants and needs in the form of privately placed insurance.

It is extremely unpopular to argue against a social security system. You are labeled a reactionary and opprobrium is heaped on you. Have you no feeling for the aged and the infirm, no charity in your heart? Sometimes we are led to wonder what ever happened to all the old people who presumably starved to death in the streets of American cities before the halcyon days of Social Security. No one seems to recall their fate.

As Goldwater learned, it was political suicide to have the temerity to suggest, ever so lightly, a voluntary system to replace the present compulsory one.

The Social Security amendments of 1965 continued the expansion and extension by creating two new programs of health insurance for the aged. The basic plan provides insurance against the expenses of hospital and related care, financed by a separate payroll tax and separate "trust" funds. The second or supplementary plan is a voluntary bargain, and provides for doctors' services, and incidentals. This latter plan is financed by small premiums, originally starting at $3.00 per month, then increased to $4.00, and further increased to $5.30 as of July 1, 1970 paid by the individual matched by a like contribution by the government. The government's share is now openly stated as coming from general revenues, the volunteer again getting something for nothing. As surely as the sun rises, politicians will vociferously vie with each other to expand medicare benefits. Then the $5.30 monthly charge will quickly and inevitably be increased from time to time. They will pass the buck to future generations pursuant to the prevailing philosophy of pay out now and get the votes now, and defer the maturity of the debt as far off as possible.

Increasing contributions serve to conceal the immorality,

the ineffectiveness, and the financial unsoundness of the Social Security System. A short time after the Medicare and Medicaid programs had gotten under way, as was to be expected, headline articles in the *New York Times* followed stating: "Doctors' Fees Up as Much as 300% Under Medicare" (8/9/66) and "Upstate Areas Fear Bankruptcy From Rising Cost of Medicaid" (9/17/67). Social Security Commissioner Robert Ball has already voiced concern that the benefits set up in the programs will be rapidly outdated by inevitable inflation.

At the time of the confirmation by the Senate of Wilbur J. Cohen as Secretary of the Department of Health, Education and Welfare, he was asked on May 9, 1968, about his estimate of the cost of Medicaid, which is the Federal program of medical care for the poor. In December 1967 he had estimated the annual cost of the program to the Federal Government at $1.7 billion in 5 years. Only five months later he admitted that if the law is not changed further, he would still have to revise his estimate upwards to an annual Federal cost of $2.5 billion or perhaps as high as $3 billion. Increasing contributions to the Social Security System have not brought and will not bring increased real benefits in terms of purchasing power. If inflation continues, as seems inevitable, it will be the same with benefits received under Medicare and Medicaid.

The mild reaction of the businessman to burgeoning government powers is surprising. The majority of businessmen, particularly the big ones, tend to accept the political power structure as a fact of life and they adjust accordingly. The power of the fat government purse which results in fat government contracts is wondrous to behold. This was clearly recognized back in 1956 by Samuel Lubell, a political analyst, in his book *The Future of American Politics* where he wrote:

The expansion of government to its present scale has politicalized virtually all economic life. The wages being paid most workers today are political wages, reflecting political pressures rather than anything that might be considered the normal working of supply and demand. The prices farmers receive are political prices. The profits business is earning are political profits. The savings people hold have become political savings, since their real value is subject to abrupt depreciation by political decisions.

To sum up, the Federal Government distributes Social Security and welfare benefits with great generosity but in effect it is buying votes with the poor taxpayers' own money.

In view of the fraud and chicanery practised and being practised by the government, when are the American people going to wake up and do something about it? Have they been so conditioned that they will continue to believe that their government speaking through its slick political salesmen always knows best? If this last question is answered affirmatively, then logically let us embrace socialism or communism wholeheartedly and be done with it. We can then rid ourselves of the pretense of being a capitalist society governed by the *laissez faire* principle under which entrepreneurs are encouraged to take risks in order to create more wealth and more jobs at higher pay which is what true economic security requires and instead place our destiny squarely in the hands of the Welfare State.

VII

• • • • • • • •

The Current Need
for a Golden Calf

THE concepts of the Welfare State have been very vaguely outlined. I have not seen defined the "Great Men" who will administer it. History has seen enough of "Great Men" and the results of their greatness.

Perhaps the vision of the Welfare State justifies the hardship of working for it. The Welfare State will, of course, in the very nature of things, have to be administered by "Great Men". Possibly, however, great men may not appear when they are most needed or they may shrink in size. Then what of the future and the security we have been promised by the great politicians of Party A if by some tragic turn of events the ignorant electorate should foolishly choose the small men of Party B!

Those who seek to be entrusted with the responsibility of looking after us from the cradle to the grave, will, as a general rule, come up from the political ranks. Will they suddenly become metamorphosed into extra-ordinary omniscient human beings as soon as they acquire the requisite power? What makes them supermen with the desire and ability to care for all our needs and to provide for our happiness and security in these parlous times?

Did Harry Truman become a "Great Man" on the day of Roosevelt's death? Or Johnson upon Kennedy's assassination? Was their greatness latent just waiting to be unveiled? In tones of humility they each accepted the highest office but before long their humility evaporated and was replaced by megalomania.

We should ponder well the words of John Stuart Mill in his "Essay on Representative Government:"

> A people may prefer a free government, but if, from indolence, or carelessness, or cowardice, or want of public spirit, they are unequal to the exertions necessary for preserving it; if they will not fight for it when it is directly attacked; if they can be deluded by the artifices used to cheat them out of it; if by momentary discouragement, or temporary panic, or a fit of enthusiasm for an individual, they can be induced to lay their liberties at the feet even of a great man, or trust him with powers which enable him to subvert their institutions; in all these cases they are more or less unfit for liberty; and though it may be for their good to have had it even for a short time, they are unlikely long to enjoy it.

The same thought was expressed in our time by Sir Isaiah Berlin in his classic *The Hedgehog & The Fox*. This world renowned philosopher there said:

> What are great men? They are ordinary human beings, who are ignorant and vain enough to accept responsibility for the life of society, individuals who would rather take the blame for all the cruelties, injustices, disasters justified in their name, than recognize their own insignificance and impotence in the cosmic flow which pursues its course irrespective of their wills and ideals.

We should not lose sight of the fact that Harry Truman did not have the business acumen to operate successfully a little haberdashery store. The business failed. It is interesting to contemplate the State of the Union and the world if he had been a successful merchant. Truman was a simple, local boy, a run of the mill, Friday night poker player who could cuss with the rest of the boys. Under normal circumstances he would hardly have been selected as the standard bearer of the Democratic party in a national election.

However, by a quirk of fate, Harry Truman now becomes President of the United States and is invested with awesome powers. It was he who made far-reaching economic decisions as well as the most awesome decision to drop the bomb. Many years later and while in his eighties, Truman makes a profound observation about inflation and interest rates, Wall Street quivers, the stock market collapses and reverberations are felt around the world. There is no evidence that he ever took a basic course in elementary economics or the science of political economy or money, credit, and banking. What suddenly made him an authority in so many fields?

Now I took Truman merely as an example to make a point. The same can be said about Johnson or Harding or Coolidge. Remember the latter's profound remark that "when there are a large number of men out of work there is unemployment." Or that other precious bit of Coolidge sagacity that "when a family is headed by a person who cannot work or who lacks the training or ability to command a good wage, the family is in trouble!"

What makes people place such faith in politicians? Perhaps it fulfills the crying need for worshipping a golden calf so urgently demanded by the Israelites. Let us recall a little Bible story.

Exodus tells us that when Moses went up to Mt. Sinai to get the law and the commandments, and his people thought he might not return, they assembled before Aaron, his mouthpiece or the present equivalent of press secretary, Secretary of State, etc. This was after Moses had led some 600,000 of his people out of the wilderness by way of the Red Sea, to toughen them up and give them a taste of the rigors and insecurity of free men. This was after they had long been slaves to Pharoah in the land of Egypt where incidentally they had enjoyed total security.

But the children of Israel had already murmured against Moses and Aaron who were giving them a rough time in the wilderness. The insecurity of freedom can prove at times unnerving and they said to Moses:

> Because there were no graves in Egypt, hast thou taken us away to die in the wilderness?—Would that we had died by the hand of the Lord in the land of Egypt, when we sat by the flesh-pots, when we did eat bread to the full; for ye have brought us forth into the wilderness, to kill this whole assembly with hunger.

Now Moses had been with the Lord on Sinai for forty days and forty nights and had neither eaten bread nor drank water, for there was much for him to learn, before he could impart it to his people. There is no short cut to wisdom.

The Israelites were really concerned about the inordinate delay in Moses' coming down from the mount and they said to Aaron:

> Up, make us a God who shall go before us; for as for this Moses, the man that brought us up out of the land of Egypt, we know not what is become of him.

Aaron was a pretty slick politician and he decided to give them what they wanted—a golden calf fashioned from their own ornaments of gold which he told them to bring him. The Good Book doesn't say whether a few golden rings and earrings which the Israelites brought to him to be melted down didn't stick to his own fingers, but I wouldn't be too surprised if it happened that way.

Well, at least the Israelites now had a god they could do business with face to face. Like the gods of other peoples, if you brought enough sacrifices you could expect a return—like perhaps a little Social Security, Medicare, Judicare, rent subsidy, free this, that, or the other. Those gods aren't too unreasonable as a general rule.

But this God of Moses made no such deals. All he promised Moses and his people was a land of opportunity and it was up to them to make it flow with milk and honey. He made it clear that they were getting no handouts or Social Security checks from Him.

When He saw what was going on, that the gang was worshipping the golden calf and that Aaron was giving the chosen people bread and circuses, He wanted to wipe them all out and start again. But Moses destroyed the molten calf as well as the Commandments and got Him to repent, for better or worse. For punishment He decided to let them engage in a bloody civil war and leave just a remnant of the faithful Levites for Moses to work on again. As related in Deuteronomy this time he succeeded and after forty years in the wilderness getting conditioned for freedom, he led his stiffnecked people who now behaved themselves towards the Promised Land.

The golden calf now is the Welfare State—or Big Brother. Pay your taxes, make your sacrifices, and have unquestioning faith. Do your worshipping and your prayers will be answered. The checks will roll out for everyone. Above all, do not doubt the gods in Washington, London, Moscow, etc. or the extra special supergod in the U.N. The State sees all, knows all, and has eternal life.

Unfortunately the Bible lesson has been forgotten. As George Santayana has said: "Those who can not remember the past are condemned to repeat it." The golden calf has been re-fashioned and named the State and there is no reason not to expect the same result. Whether or not there will be a remnant left this time to try again would appear to be the only question.

This need for a golden calf is an interesting phenomenon. Free men, like Americans with a heritage of liberty, have abandoned personal responsibility for their own welfare and are quite willing to delegate such responsibility to strange men called collectively Government or the State. They have developed the pernicious habit of rushing to their government to solve all their problems expecting a political solution for all the ills man is heir to. They abdicate their personal responsibilities and the point has now been reached that the all powerful, omniscient State has become the repository of all the wisdom of all the people. The illusion persists that the ballot effectively controls the State. What really happens, however, is that while the politicans come and go, the State grows and remains more powerful and more entrenched than ever. The people have given up on their own quest for security and these strangers whom they elect willingly accept the responsibility under the assumption that there is a political solution for any and all problems. It matters not that these men are in general wholly unqualified by training and experience for such a heavy burden. Nevertheless, these presumably super humans embodied in the concept of the State are in some mysterious fashion expected to do for us what they have not been able to accomplish for themselves. Somehow the whole has the synergistic effect of becoming greater than the sum of its parts. It is indeed a puzzlement.

VIII

· · · · · · · · ·

The Effects of Inflation

THE dictionary definition of security is—

> The state or feeling of being free from fear, care, danger etc; safety or a sense of safety, freedom from doubt; certainty.

The slave was secure—so is the prisoner, especially if he is confined for life. No cares, no worries, no taxes, all his belly wants taken care of, free medical care, and a roof over his head. Total security.

If this is the aim of the "Welfare State," it should be frankly stated. However, we find that the Welfare State and security are not synonymous.

While we are on the subject of definition, we might as well define the phrase "Welfare State" used so extensively throughout the world. The term evokes deep emotions and it is interesting to note that it cannot be traced in print further back than 1947. An excellent definition and one which conforms to the general understanding of the expression in both academic and political circles is that by Walter Hagenbuch, the Cambridge economist. He defines it as "a society in which every citizen is provided by the State with services that ensure economic security for himself and his family". It is this sentiment that is embodied in Social Security legislation in America.

A short time after President Nixon took office, he asked his top domestic policy advisors to explore a very perplexing phenomenon. What, he wanted to know, accounted for the explosive increase in the nation's relief rolls during the time that his predecessor kept reminding us that "we never had it so good".

President Nixon found that unemployment was indeed around its lowest point since the Korean War. Nevertheless, despite the billions of dollars being poured into new programs designed to fight the war against poverty, the relief rolls kept rising at the rate of about 10% a year. As he took the oath of office, New York City alone had a million people on relief. His experts were just as puzzled as he was and no one was able to explain the riddle to him.

Since this chapter is concerned with the effects of inflation on our economy in general and on the purchasing power of Social Security pensions in particular, it would be wise to define that term also. We recognize inflation when we see it in operation so the definition should be relatively easy.

Economists do not differ greatly in telling us what inflation is. We are told it is "too many dollars chasing too few goods." Many define it as "a substantial and persistent increase in the general price level".

Recipients of Social Security complain bitterly that their checks buy less and less as they grow older. While the checks may be social in nature, they afford no security to the retiree. Periodic increases of basic Social Security benefits never quite catch up with inflation, proposed mechanisms for automatic cost-of-living adjustments notwithstanding.

The dollar has lost about 50 percent of its purchasing power in the last 20 years. However, Americans are relatively speaking quite fortunate. The situation is much worse in England and France. In some South American countries practically the whole value of people's savings—92 to 95 cents in every dollar—has been wiped out by inflation in the last 10 years. This includes countries with the most advanced and liberal Social Security programs designed to bring security to the retired worker.

Since 1940, over 60 percent of all life insurance, pension reserves, and savings deposits in America have been confiscated by this subtle process of inflation. The purchasing power of the dollar has decreased at an average rate of 3½ percent. In 1968 prices rose at the rate of more than 4%; in 1969 the rate was over 6%. In 1970, it may be higher.

Millions of Americans who tried to provide for their own retirement or for the care of their dependents have already seen what was to have been an adequate income coupled with Social Security payments lose all but a fraction of its buying power. Now instead of being financially independent—if the wizards in Washington had left things alone—they find themselves dependent on these same geniuses and the Welfare State for belated pitiful increases in Social Security pensions that make up for a small part of the lost buying power of their accumulated savings.

Lenin predicted that inflation would defeat the capitalist countries rather than military conquest. Inflation played a vital part in the Russian revolution. We have seen that it accounted for the rise of Hitler in Germany and it reduced France to a second-rate nation. Inflation's destructive power has been amply demonstrated historically and it is currently eroding the foundation of the American economic system and creating a prevalent feeling of insecurity.

Security for certain individuals was no myth before the

advent of the Welfare State. Americans worked hard, saved for a rainy day, built or bought their own homes, paid off mortgages, bought life insurance and annuities at a constantly expanding rate, built, bought and invested in businesses as entrepreneurs, accumulated capital which was either used by themselves or which they loaned to others in exchange for interest which the borrowers were glad to pay, and in many other ways planned and provided for their retirement.

Contrast the security obtained in this fashion by an individual for himself, with that promised and delivered by Social Security.

The current recipients of Social Security payments who have contributed for thirty years know now that it is impossible to retire, completely dependent on these Social Security payments. Since Social Security benefits were first paid out in 1940, they have been raised 7 times. But the larger number of dollars paid out buy less today in purchasing power than they did in 1940. Inflation, created and spawned by our great benefactor, the Welfare State, robs the worker of the benefits of the greater production he has achieved with the cooperation of advancing capitalist technology.

The benefits of greater productivity are cancelled by the heavy hand of the State in the exercise of its taxing powers. For example, The Tax Foundation, a non-profit organization, conservatively estimates that there are over 151 taxes hidden in one loaf of bread. Further estimates of the number of hidden taxes on some basic necessities of life from raw material supplier to retailer are as follows:

Egg	— Over 100 hidden taxes
Man's suit	— Over 116 hidden taxes
House	— Over 600 hidden taxes.

Just as the Medicare program got under way in 1966, Social Security Commissioner Ball was worried that inflation might make it unworkable. He attacked the symptoms of inflation instead of the cause by suggesting that benefits be tied to a cost-of-living index to make Medicare inflation proof. The same plan has been under study in connection with Social Security payments. The Doctor prefers treating the disease symptomatically by periodic increases in Social Security payments since each time these payments are raised, the Doctor and his cohorts get a lot of publicity and automatic adjustments are thus dispensed with as unnecessary. Furthermore, these cost-of-living adjustments would not affect private pension plans covering millions of workers who are hurt by inflation just as much as the Social Security beneficiaries are.

Ironically, it was the Social Security Commissioner's own government, with its monetary and fiscal excesses, that was and is primarily responsible for creating the inflation that disturbed him with respect to Medicare and has upset the plans of those thrifty Americans who tried to care for their own needs in their old age. Inflation is a tricky way of extracting dollars from the taxpayer without his feeling it directly. The Social Security System aids and abets that deceit, and serves to enhance the power of taxation to destroy private enterprise and the capitalist system.

Millions of these workers who have been thrifty and provided the capital for an expanding economy hoped that with their savings and investments supplemented by their Social Security payments they could take care of themselves in their retirement years. To their sorrow, they found that instead of gaining financial independence they are more and more dependent on their Government for increases in Social Security pensions to in some small measure compensate for the lost buying power of their other assets.

To cite some examples of how the American public is

beguiled by Social Security promises let us look at some case histories. For example, a worker and his wife who retired in 1940 could have received up to $68.40 monthly. If both were still living in 1968, the latest increase in Social Security benefits would have raised their monthly check to $198.25. But because of inflation their $198.25 in 1968 would be worth only $67.08 in 1940 dollars—in other words, their benefit would buy less than their 1940 check.

Take another case history of a man and his wife who retired in 1950 at the highest possible actual benefit of $120.00 monthly. The following table shows the increases the couple would have received over the years and the purchasing power of the benefits based upon the 1950 dollar. The table shows clearly that each increase came at a time when purchasing power of the monthly benefit was below (or threatened to dip below) the level of the 1950 benefit.

Social Security Benefits for a Worker and His Wife Who Retired in 1950

Year	Actual Maximum Monthly Benefit in Dollars	Purchasing Power of Benefit in 1950 dollars
1950	$120.00	$120.00
1951	120.00	111.15
1952	127.50	115.44
1953	127.50	114.47
1954	147.70	132.24
1955	147.70	132.49
1956	147.70	130.63
1957	147.70	126.30
1958	147.70	122.96
1959	157.50	129.94

1960	157.50	128.08
1961	157.50	126.50
1962	157.50	125.20
1963	157.50	123.61
1964	157.50	122.02
1965	157.50	120.03

In an article in "Economic News" for January 1963, published by the American Institute for Economic Research, entitled "Anything France Can Do We Can Do Better!", it was demonstrated most graphically that the French experience with inflation in the 40 years between 1915–1955 is being duplicated in America with alarming precision from 1940 to the date of the article.

We can see from the chart and the corresponding figures extended to date that as a matter of startling fact, in relation to the purchasing power of 1940 dollars, the dollar today is worth less than 41¢. In 1974, judging from the present rate of decline it will be worth about 25¢. By the 1980's it will be worth 1¢, having lost 99% of its purchasing power by then, in a little over 40 years.

Inflation is rampant and the erosion of the purchasing power of the dollar continues to pick up speed. The *New York Times* of August 23, 1966, in a front page article, reported that consumer prices continued their steady rise for July 1966 as reported by the United States Labor Department and marked 1966 as the most inflationary year since 1957.

Based on that report, a 1966 dollar was worth 42¢ as compared to the dollar of 1940. The following table shows dramatically what has happened up to 1970. The source is the United States Bureau of Labor Statistics: (all figures are the average for each year)

Purchasing Power of Dollar
1940 = $1.00

1940	$1.00
1941	.95
1942	.86
1943	.81
1944	.80
1945	.78
1946	.72
1947	.63
1948	.58
1949	.59
1950	.58
1951	.54
1952	.53
1953	.52
1954	.52
1955	.52
1956	.52
1957	.50
1958	.49
1959	.48
1960	.47
1961	.47
1962	.46
1963	.46
1964	.45
1965	.44
1966	.42
1967	.41
1968	.40
1969	.37

Is there any likelihood of a reversal of the trend, with all the welfare plans in the offing plus the inflation flowing from the war in Viet Nam and the way it is being financed?

Perhaps, then, security is not all it is cracked up to be. Are there any good things to be said for insecurity?

It has been seen that the prisoner and the slave are quite willing to trade their security for the hazards of insecurity that accompany freedom. The great achievements of mankind, the discoveries and voyages into the unknown, the challenges and responses to greater heights were all benefits flowing from trading the secure for the insecure. A life free of all problems, hazards, and uncertainties may prove to be quite deadly and boring.

The driving force of insecurity for the individual, and the rewards that would inure to his benefit and indirectly to society in general, from his efforts to be relatively less insecure, may well be the spirit that has made America the greatest world power today. Slaves are shielded from the responsibility of making decisions, taking risks and responding to challenges. We must choose between the security of slavery and the liberty and insecurity of free men. We can't have both.

The ideal society has been pictured for us as one in which every one wakes up in the morning with a smile on his face, a song in his heart, money in his pocket, two chickens in every pot, 2 cars in every garage, no problems, no tensions, no responsibilities, and all of this made possible by the wisdom of the super-men who have it in their power to so order happiness and security.

The promises by big government of security by assuming more power thereby enabling it to take care of all its citizens from the cradle to the grave resulted in the decline and fall of Athens and Rome in ancient times, as well as Britain in our time. When men are beguiled into trading individual liberty for a state-guaranteed Social Security pension they will lose their individual liberty and the chance to provide for their own security, and at the same time will become pawns and slaves of the state. Their security so obtained will be slave-oriented and entirely dependent upon the whim and caprice of their masters. No person can ever really depend for his security upon a promise or gift from another, whether a private person or a politician. The only true security lies in the individual himself, if the rules of the game are correctly delineated and Big Daddy keeps his hands off.

Real security will have a chance when the time comes that the citizenry will say to their government "Don't give me anything. I know you have nothing of your own to give me and your promises to bear gifts can only be fulfilled if you first appropriate what belongs to someone else, or better still what you will take or have already taken from me in the first place. I well know that all you want is my vote and so hope to perpetuate yourself in power. I am not that stupid. If you let me alone, and permit me to work and provide for my own security under favorable conditions, you may get my vote, but not if you keep promising me something for nothing."

The politicians should be treated with derision and contempt when their actions warrant it as is most often the case. I don't think the American taxpayer by any stretch of the imagination has authorized the expenditure of his hard earned money to learn why Australian aborigines sweat or why ostriches in Africa behave the way they do, or to discover the details of the love life of an octopus. The extraction of these extra billions in taxes from the pay envelopes of the lowest income groups, not for the funding of social insurance but for government expenditures hardly related directly or indirectly to the war effort, must have a depressive effect upon the already limited purchasing power of these low income taxpayers and on the entire economy.

Unfortunately and mysteriously the adulation of the State by its citizens persists and grows. The State has the means to manage the news and does so in order to convince the taxpayer of its supreme wisdom. As of this writing, each month twenty-five- million Americans receive checks from the Social Security Administration amounting to over 2 billion dollars. Both the Democrats and the Republicans are falling over themselves in their promises to expand the size of these checks and wherever possible to increase the number of the recipients. After all, will we bite the hand that feeds us? Unless we soon start biting, or at the very least start snarling, it will be too late.

The Social Security System has now become the personal plaything of whoever happens to be in the White House at any given time and is the device by which those on the outside looking in, seek to oust the current incumbent. If there were ever a case of a direct pandering for votes, this is it.

Where the people have grown accustomed to the principle of private ownership of property as they have in America, and the right of the individual to keep what he has produced, it is not politically expedient for any government in power to insist upon too much direct taxation or it just won't get the votes. The majority will not go for it. It might look better for the record to try to reach the property of the very wealthy by direct taxes, since their relatively few votes are not too important. However just let the powers that be try to dig more heavily into such property as may be owned by those citizens who constitute the voting majority! No politician rides into power on his promises of increasing taxes on the masses. If the government expects to take a very high proportion of national income, it will always search for methods of raising revenue which are more ingenious than direct taxation. The language and approach of the Social Security tax is loaded with just that kind of ingenuity and deviousness.

There are not too many ways left to get additional substantial tax revenues to satiate the appetite of the Federal Government and the Social Security tax bite is becoming of increasing importance in that respect as will be demonstrated at great length in a later chapter.

It is interesting to note that it is not due to bad times or in a period of large scale unemployment that the so-called Anti-Poverty program is launched as part and parcel of the Great Society, and continued under President Nixon.

As this page is being written, there are 58 full pages of "Help Wanted" advertisements in the *New York Times*. It is common for over 100 pages of similar ads to appear in the Los Angeles Times. These two cities are by no means unique and the shortage of labor at good dollar wages is acute in America.

Nevertheless the standard cliches roll on that Big Brother is lying awake nights worrying about his flock and how to solve the unemployment problem. I revert to President Johnson's speech of April 8, 1966, where he said:

> I would like for our individuals now on welfare rolls to be provided additional incentives for them to find work.

Do the unemployed or recipients of welfare need any more incentive than to look into the help-wanted columns of their daily newspaper? There are innumerable cases where it doesn't pay the unemployed to take a job at $100.00 per week, when Federal, State and often city income taxes plus Social Security taxes, taken out of their pay envelope leaves little more in it than the unemployment insurance check (tax free) would represent.

In 1946 Senator Robert A. Taft introduced a bill that provided for matching grants to states for medical care for all those who could pass a means test establishing that they were indigent and unable to pay for their own medical care. At the hearings organized labor was represented by William Green, president of the American Federation of Labor who testified and summed up his opposition to the proposed legislation by saying "The workers of this country are not prepared to accept the pauper's oath as the approach to better health." Paraphrasing the famous slogan "rather death than dishonor" in effect he proposed that the worker would rather be sick than use his own money to pay to be restored to good health.

When we get down to the question then of defining who are the needy, apparently the fact that a person has enough money to take care of his own medical bills, under the prevailing spirit of the times, should not disqualify him from receiving a government handout for that purpose. Today a means test is considered demeaning. If an eccentric millionaire chooses to ride the gravy train too, who shall deny him a free ride? After all nobody pays for anything anyway. Through Social Security we can all live in retirement in a sunny land surrounded by senior citizens similarly disposed, by the simple process of taking in each other's wash.

Before Social Security, assistance to the needy was financed primarily by local government. At the local level, public opinion, aside from legal requirements, caused close relatives to look after those in real need. In addition aid when needed was and still is rendered by community religious and charitable organizations. It was not considered degrading to have children look after their parents and possibly siblings care for each other, rather than have a stranger do so. Now, however, there seems to be nothing dishonorable in accepting public charity under the aegis of Social Security. To realize just how phony the whole set-up is we need only refer to the Social Security amendment giving monthly checks to everyone who reaches the magic age of 72, even if he never contributed one cent. Here was a group of voters, at the last count about 700 thousand of them, who had not yet received a hand-out so why not buy them off too and put them in the right camp? Politics makes strange bedfellows and 700 thousand old bedfellows also vote.

It is because of these abuses of the taxpayers' money that our government has been converted into a giant Santa Claus. In the old days, the local ward-heeler took care of his constituents by giving them free turkeys on Thanksgiving and the like. Our current breed of politician in Washington are more sophisticated and their hand-outs in exchange for votes are far more extensive but the underlying principle is the same and now everyone wants to ride the gravy train.

A case in point is the proliferation of private pension plans. At present about 50 percent of the working population are covered by such plans. According to economist Roger F. Murray of the Teachers Insurance and Annuity Association, by 1980 the number protected is expected to be 60 percent and the assets $193 billion. Andrew Brown of the United Auto Workers covering the largest group of industrial workers says "The auto worker today can retire with over $5000 —a year, counting his pension and Social Security". When we consider that very often retired couples own their own home, such a sum would normally be ample for their retirement needs.

Inflation has been most extreme in personal services. A leading hospital administrator told his audience at a California medical convention that in about 30 years or by the year 2000, a semi-private room in a hospital would cost $300 a day. This prediction brought a response from a University of California professor that the estimate was much too low as he projected the results of inflation.

All Ponzi schemes inevitably collapse. The Social Security promises constantly being made by the party in power as well as the party seeking reinstatement, are no exception. Since no political party can afford to or dare to renege on those promises, and since in America both major political parties are equally to blame, the political solution will be to let runaway inflation erode the value of the pension dollars. The 25 million Social Security checks will go out regularly on the same day of each month, but the recipients unfortunately will find very little security value in those inflated dollars.

IX

• • • • • • • •

The Arithmetic of
Social Security

THE justification for Social Security is based on the humanitarian concept that financial distress in old-age, poverty and illness can and should be alleviated by the Government. The Government assumes that the individual does not have the knowledge and experience to make a sensible allocation of his income so as to satisfy firstly his basic minimal needs, and then to decide how much to allocate or spend for luxuries, and how much to set aside for savings for his own old-age, and make reasonable provisions for his dependents in the event of his disability or death.

It is interesting to note in this connection that Americans, even young ones, are quite concerned with protecting their dependents. The amount of life insurance in force with United States life insurance companies is over $1 trillion and the commitment by these companies to pay off is amply funded. Two out of every three Americans own some form of life insurance, the average new policy amounting to $9,-000.00. Nine out of every ten husbands under 65 own some kind of life insurance having a face value averaging $11,-

400.00. Apparently Americans realize the inadequacy of the purchasing power of Social Security payments and and in 1966 bought an all-time record total of $121 billion worth of life insurance, more than double the amount they had purchased ten years earlier. This would seem to contradict the rationale for Social Security that Americans have neither the concern nor the ability to look after themselves.

The family breadwinner usually buys an insurance policy to protect his wife and children. However, if in the year 1970 a man 25 years old gets married, and 25 years later dies after having raised his children who are now emancipated, his widow as the law now stands will get a monthly benefit of exactly zero for his payment of all those Social Security taxes for 25 years. She will have to live at least another 10 years before she collects a dime. All she gets upon his death is a lump sum death benefit not to exceed $255.00 to help defray his funeral cost. If his widow should die 10 years after his death, the Government will have collected thousands of dollars in payroll taxes from the deceased and his employer under the guise of "insurance" premiums and will not have to pay a cent to the "policy holder" or his beneficiary. If the worker happens to be a bachelor or a widower with no dependents on his 65th birthday and dies shortly thereafter, the Government may have collected over $50,000 (excluding interest) in his Social Security "account" and his heirs if not dependent on him get nothing nor can he dispose of his Social Security Account" in his last Will and Testament.

There are many competing forces seeking to gain a preference when each of us has to do his arithmetic with his earnings. In spending his income, choices have to be made daily whether to purchase meat or fish, new shoes or re-sole the old ones, eat at home or in a restaurant, and if the decision is to splurge, whether to go all out or be modest, order caviar or ham and eggs, champagne or beer. Savings banks urge you to save, life insurance companies urge you to buy insurance to protect your family, mutual funds have one approach, stockbrokers another. The Government says buy its bonds. Finance companies urge you to borrow, the airlines say fly now-pay later. Life is pretty complicated but it was ever thus since man's desires are unlimited and never satisfied.

If the income is too low, it is recognized that providing food, clothing and shelter makes it impossible to put anything aside for old-age retirement. Unfortunately, under the Social Security System, the poorest worker is compelled to save for his old-age even if in the process he must go hungry. He may not earn enough to pay an income tax and is classified with his family as below the poverty line, but nevertheless each payday his envelope is tapped for his old-age pension. Some other countries have recognized this inequity by exempting small incomes from Social Security taxes depending on the size of the family unit, just like income tax exemptions.

The unskilled worker who first enters the Social Security System is generally quite young around 18. However, the more affluent who finish college, and perhaps take graduate work thereafter, or who become professionals, may not contribute to Social Security until perhaps ten years later. Of course, as a general rule, they are financially well to do with no need for Social Security, but despite their delayed status as Social Security cardholders, they will enjoy virtually the same benefits at retirement age with the poor kid who started to work at 17 and may pay in thousands of dollars more than the doctor or engineer. This discrimination can easily be over-come even under the presently constituted Social Security System by simply exempting all under 25 years of age from this tax.

Now getting back to our arithmetic. The Government also

can figure and get its share first. Social Security taxes designed to finance the seven percent retroactive boost in Social Security benefits and the start of the Medicare program from July 1, 1966, shot up on January 1, 1966. In addition to an increase in the tax rate, the taxable wage base itself was raised from the first $4800.00 of wages to the first $6600.00. Due to inflation and the successive wage boosts obtained in an attempt to keep up with the constantly rising cost of living, many more workers were earning considerably above the $4800.00 level. Here was an additional source of tax money readily available, and the purveyors of the "Great Society" did not let it go untapped for very long. Again effective January 1, 1968, the base was raised 20 percent to $7800. And the tax rate also was increased to where it reaches 11.8 percent in 1987.

There was a sixty percent increase in Social Security taxes from 1965 to 1966, purportedly intended to finance the hike in Social Security benefits and the beginning of the Medicare program. The history of Social Security taxes is following the same pattern of the income tax. Start in a small way, get your foot in the door, and gradually the taxpayer will become anaesthetized and helpless, and won't even realize what is happening to him.

Since Social Security started in 1937 there have been 17 tax and/or wage base increases. Although benefits have been increased 119 percent the Social Security taxes have increased 480 percent. Since 1949 the tax rate, shared equally by both employees and employers has increased over 260 percent. Under the 1967 amendments effective January 1, 1968, the increase since 1949 would amount to 435 percent by 1973. In addition, as previously noted, the principle of using general Treasury funds instead of the "trust" funds for Social Security payments has already been established. Old age pensions for 72 year old people, who never paid a penny for their pensions, are being paid out of general revenues which also are the source of half the cost of the voluntary medicare program for paying doctors' bills.

When Senator Ribicoff was Secretary of Health, Education and Welfare and at the time the taxable wage base was still $4800.00, we recall that he stated that a total ten percent Social Security tax was probably the practical maximum that could or should ever be reached. The ten percent take and more after 1970 on all annual wages up to $7800.00 has already been legalized, and the increases already scheduled by Congress will make it 11.3% by 1973 and on a taxable base raised from $6600.00 to $7800.00 of annual wages. If you want to bet on a sure thing, make a wager that the base will go up before many years have passed.

In the whopping proposals proposed by President Johnson and by Congress, a nice new package, gift-wrapped, was delivered to Americans before they went to the polls in 1968. This provided overall increases in benefits as well as sharply increased minimum benefits. It has been stated by the Department of Health, Education and Welfare that the projected "surplus" in the Social Security "Trust fund" would pay for about half of the gift, the other half coming as a result of increasing the wage base subject to Social Security taxes. It didn't save the election for the Democrats, however.

When Washington agreed to pay for one-half of New York State's Medicaid program, that State passed its Medicaid bill. This contained the most generous eligibility requirements. Any family of 4 persons earning less than $6000 a year as its take home pay was entitled to full medical benefits.

You didn't have to be a genius to predict that this was ridiculous and couldn't last very long. The costs, of course, became unmanageable and the Federal Government amended the Medicaid Law and New York thereupon cut back its eligibility provisions in order to qualify under the Federal program. In its first year of operation, Medicaid cost more than 5 times the original Government estimate of $247 million.

We have seen that these constantly expanding benefits being promised by the government to those compelled to contribute to Social Security, rests practically exclusively upon its power to tax workers not yet on the collecting end enough to pay off those retiring from the work force. The only way to make good on the promise is to tax current production. The so-called trust fund mentioned in government literature is empty except for receipts or I.O.U.'s Uncle Sam put in the cash register as a record showing how much he spent for current and past operating expenses of one kind or another.

Of course, these I.O.U.'s or government bonds are a charge on future production before even the workers destined for retirement in the future can expect to be paid. The bonds will be redeemed or the bond-holders will extend the time of the debtor to make good. The debt and interest will be paid off by taxing workers again in dollars of constantly decreasing purchasing power, which is the only possible way the tremendous debt can be handled.

No one really knows how much the government owes now. To the national debt must be added all the other government obligations like accruing Social Security benefits, FHA debentures, benefits promised to farmers, subsidies and other commitments to the shipping industry, Civil Service Retirement needs, contingent liabilities on all sorts of guarantees, etc. The other liabilities have conservatively been estimated as high as a trillion dollars. The first Actuary of the Social Security Board, Mr. W.R. Williamson, estimated in 1961 that projected payments to living taxpayers in the Social Security System and their dependents came to about $1.5 trillion and that the "on-paper" Trust Fund, so called, would cover about one percent. It is difficult to imagine a more hopelessly insolvent debtor than Uncle Sam. If he filed a petition in bankruptcy now, and his assets were marshalled to pay off his liabilities it is extremely doubtful if creditors would realize 1¢ on the dollar for their claims.

It is at the same time extremely unlikely that any government would renege on promised Social Security benefits. It has a more sophisticated way of defaulting. The dollars will be forthcoming to the beneficiaries as promised but they will be five or ten cent dollars as far as real purchasing power is concerned. There will be very little security in those social security dollars as present beneficiaries are unfortunately realizing. It should be pointed out, in this connection, that unlike a contract or policy with an insurance company, Congress retains the absolute unilateral right at any time to alter the deal. It can raise or reduce the benefits, and at will can also increase the Social Security tax and the taxable base as it has in the past, or as is most unlikely, reduce the taxes and the base upon which they operate. The taxpayer has no legal, binding contract with the government but only a moral claim. This was decided in the case of *Fleming* v. *Nestor*, 363 U.S. 603 (1960) which approved of the constitutionality of a provision which forbids Social Security benefits to persons deported for subversive activies, despite the fact that such activities took place before the provision had been enacted. The Supreme Court decided that the "OASI program is in no sense a federally-administered 'insurance program' under which each worker pays 'premiums' over the years and acquires at retirement an indefeasible right." More on the Nestor case in Chapter X.

One example of a change Congress made detrimental to the taxpayer took place in 1939. When Social Security was enacted in 1935, it was provided that no one could lose under the system and that at least the taxpayer or his estate would get back what he paid. If a taxpayer became 65 without having qualified by having been in the system for a sufficient number of quarters, he would still get his money back. Also in that case, upon his death, his estate would get the refund. If a pensioner while collecting, died before he collected at least what he had paid in, his estate or family would get the difference. There were about 500,000 such refunds. In 1939, Congress changed its mind and cancelled such benefits, making it crystal clear that the taxpayer has no contract with the government, which can alter, cancel or modify the so-called guaranty at any time and however it chooses. Now the estate of a worker who dies before retirement, leaving no dependents qualified to draw survivors' benefits, gets a modest benefit of $255 and nothing else.

Congress did the same dishonest thing in the Social Security Amendment of 1967 when it made some significant changes in the provisions of the Social Security Administration relating to old-age benefits to non-citizens of the United States residing outside of the country. This again proved beyond a doubt that the right to Social Security benefits is not a contractual obligation of the American Government with the taxpayer. An insurance policy providing for an annuity for the policy holder does not depend on his residence. When the payment is due under his contract, the company will mail his monthly check to him wherever he resides. This used to be the law with reference to Social Security payments too. But since July 1, 1968, the right to benefits no longer depends on whether you earned and were entitled to your old-age pension. The 1967 Social Security Amendments change the definition of what constitutes absence from the United States; they alter the treatment of citizens of some countries that do not meet the social insurance or pension system exception; and they alter the treatment of non-citizens of the United States residing in countries covered by Treasury regulations which prohibit mailing payments to beneficiaries residing in certain countries. The poor worker doesn't even get his own money back and the powerful United States Government is thereby unjustly enriched by those paltry sums.

Private voluntary annuity contracts and a large number of private retirement plans provide that payment of the annuity begins at a certain specified age whether or not the insured person retires. They further provide that if for any reason retirement is deferred after the specified age the amount of annuity to be paid on actual retirement is increased proportionately and substantially in many cases depending on how long retirement is deferred.

Another important distinction between the Social Security System and a voluntary plan, is that under the latter, the individual can adjust his affairs to meet his own needs. He might decide to take his annuity at 65 to enable him to take it easy and earn less. Or he might decide to continue to work as before and take a much larger annuity later on to enable him to live at the same standard after complete retirement. The choice is entirely his. We are now recognizing that for many people, working after 65 gives them greater satisfaction and keeps them mentally and physically alert and in better health than retirement. Under Social Security as presently constituted the worker is penalized for continuing to work after retirement age. A man of 72 or over still working while receiving Social Security benefits, must continue to pay Social Security taxes.

Another subtle deception is embodied in the technique of

extracting taxes via Social Security payments. By virtue of the payroll-withholding, the worker does not get to see or handle the tax he is compelled to pay. If he had his hands on that five percent plus the five percent the boss pays it might dawn on him that he could get a much better annuity from a solvent insurance company. The small size of the increases in Social Security taxes extracted from the pay envelope over the last thirty years has enabled the deception to be accomplished without any furor.

When the government collects the Social Security tax from the employer, the worker is deceived into thinking that the share the boss pays comes out of his own pocket and is used to help finance the worker's pension or retirement fund. The truth is that in effect the worker is paying both halves. For an employer to stay in business, whether it be General Motors, United States Steel, or the corner grocer, he must recover his cost of production which is included in the price of his product as it gets to the market place.

If the employer's payroll tax is five percent or fifty percent, it will be included in the cost of his product and thus serve to further reduce the purchasing power of the dollar. Of course, the illusion that the employer is contributing one-half of the cost of the special retirement fund held in a sacred trust by the government, is, euphemistically speaking, another stroke of political genius, or to be honest and blunt, simply political chicanery.

The worker may or may not realize that the share his employer pays is in reality almost entirely being paid by him also out of his production. Competition would have compelled the employer to pay his share as part of the cost of labor either as higher pay to his employees or in reduced prices to consumers. This is true whether we assume that the tax is passed on and added to the price of the goods or services or is shifted backward resulting in lower wages.

This was recognized as far back as 1941 when Professor Seymour Harris wrote in Economics of Social Security (pp. 285–286):

> Economists who, in the years preceding the introduction of the Social Security Act, had given the problem of incidence careful consideration, seem to have been in general agreement that a payroll tax, whether levied on the worker or the employer, would be paid ultimately by the workers. * * * In the years that have passed since the Social Security Act became law, the weight of informed opinion still seems to be that the payroll tax is borne largely by the workers."

The employer doesn't care whether he pays his workers a weekly wage of $100.00 + $5.00 for Social Security or the whole $105.00 directly to them. He knows his labor cost in either event is the same. Ordinarily he would prefer putting $105.00 directly into the pay envelope but he has no choice. If that $5.00 bill did not have to be paid by the employer, competition would have extracted it from him anyway, either in higher current wages to his employees or reflected in the form of lower prices to consumers. No matter how you figure it, in its ultimate effect, the employee carries the entire burden of the Social Security taxes, his own and the matching contributed nominally paid by his employer.

Even the Social Security Administration admits that the employer's share of the tax is borne ultimately, if not entirely, at least substantially by the worker. It observed:

> Even though it is true that the employer contribution in the final analysis is borne in considerable part by employees, either because they receive lower wages than they otherwise would or because as consumers they pay higher prices than

they otherwise would, it does not follow that the incidence of the employer tax falls on wage earners in exact proportion to the earnings on which the tax is paid. The incidence of the tax will depend in specific instances on a variety of complex factors. The employer tax, therefore, may be looked on as being for the use of the system as a whole, and not as a matching contribution that is to be credited to each particular employee on the basis of the amount he paid. (President's Proposals for Revision of the Social Security System—hearings before the Committee on Ways and Means 3/1/2 and 3, 1967)

It doesn't soften the blow much to allege that the employer's share is destined "for the use of the system as a whole" since it would be destined for the worker's own pay envelope as he is responsible for earning it.

Under the present law enacted and effective in 1968 the workers' share of the Social Security tax is scheduled to rise in certain stages and reach $460.20 by 1987. Added to the employers' share the Government will get $920.40 attributable to each covered employee in Social Security "contributions" in addition to all of its other taxes and levies. If the base is enlarged as it undoubtedly will be, the combined Social Security tax will be well over $1,000 a year.

The deception has been so thoroughly exposed by now, that few people in or out of government seriously contend that what we are discussing is really an "insurance" or pension plan pursuant to which workers set aside a part of their earnings for their retirement. The figures clearly reveal that under present and projected schedules, the discounted values of the promised benefits will never equal or exceed the Social Security taxes paid plus nominal interest. A few years ago the esteemed economist Professor Milton Friedman of the University of Chicago characterized the set-up as a "raw deal" for the youngster just starting to work. In an article in *Newsweek* (4/3/67) entitled "On Social Security" he said:

> Retired persons currently enjoy a bonanza. But youngsters currently entering the system are getting a raw deal. * * * To finance the excess payments to the growing number of retired, taxes have had to be raised repeatedly. As a result the benefits promised younger workers are much smaller than the equivalent of the taxes paid on their wages.

The Social Security tax is beginning to look like a most important source for satisfying the constantly growing appetite of the government. In 1945, for example, Social Security collections represented only 2.9 per cent of total Federal tax receipts. Twenty years later it was about 20 per cent and in fiscal 1968 the Treasury estimated it will account for close to 25 per cent of all tax receipts. It is now a larger source of revenue for the Federal Government than even corporation income taxes and is exceeded only by receipts from individual income taxes.

Another vicious feature of the Social Security Tax, very rarely discussed, is its manifest unfairness to those wage earners in the lower brackets. While it is becoming a major source of government funds, it is burdening the poor disproportionately. An identical rate applies to all taxpayers rich or poor up to a certain maximum of annual earnings, now $7,800. Above $7,800 the wage earner pays nothing and the tax is less as a proportion of annual earnings as the earnings increase above the base subject to Social Security taxes. It is clearly a regressive tax. In addition, there are no deductions from either the percentage withheld or the base. Neither sickness, nor dependents, no casualty, catastrophe, or misfortune will reduce your Social Security tax. At least in the income tax there are some provisions like those mentioned which may serve to soften the blow. Under Social Security there are no exemptions whatsoever, and to that extent there are virtually no opportunities for tax avoidance. It also places a greater burden on families with more than one worker which is becoming the rule due to the high cost of living.

For example, a man earning $150.00 per week, under the 1968 rates would pay 4.4% of his income for Social Security taxes or $6.60. A man earning twice as much would still pay the same $6.60 or only 2.2% of his annual income. The greater the income the smaller the tax rate. In many cases the payroll tax ostensibly designed to finance Social Security exceeds the income tax of the worker.

It should also be noted that in America, Social Security taxes are not deductible as they are in some other countries in arriving at taxable income so that in effect the worker is forced to pay a tax upon a tax. The Social Security tax is extracted from his pay envelope before he gets to touch it and his income to the extent of his Social Security tax is taxed again when he files his annual income tax returns.

Social Security Commissioner Robert M. Ball was quoted as saying "a worker will get back in benefits about what he puts into the system from his own earnings." The fallacy and delusion in his statement is apparent when we realize that the worker is not going to put his Social Security money in his mattress for safekeeping. Even if he only put it in a savings account he would get compounded interest of 5%. If he were a little more venturesome perhaps he might have even bought some IBM stock or other securites with his accumulated Social Security taxes. In either event he would get back a lot more than what he put into the Social Security taxes. Adding further insult to the injury of the poor taxpayer is the fact that Mr. Ball neglects to mention the steady erosion of the purchasing power of the worker's dollars over the years before he eventually starts collecting his social security pension.

We have seen that despite successive tax rises and an enlarged tax base, Social Security payments buy less now in real dollars than when the program started some thirty-four years ago. There is no reason to doubt as we see what is going on about us, that inflationary tendencies are very much at work and that this trend will persist in the foreseeable future.

In the millions of booklets published by the Social Security Administration in January 1968 entitled "Recent Improvements in your Social Security " explaining the 1967 Social Security Amendments, there was set forth the following chart:

The penultimate sentence in the small print in the footnote should be kept in mind as these maximum benefits based on average yearly earnings of $7800 would not be payable for many many years to come. Since the $7800 base did not become effective until 1968, a current taxpayer cannot attain that average earnings base to entitle him to the maximum retirement benefit of $218 a month set forth in the chart until the 21st century rolls around which fact his Government artfully neglects to mention when it naively states in this 1968 brochure that these benefits "generally will not be payable until later". The use of the word "generally" is an absolute fraud calculated to deceive and the word "later" is definitely misleading. Even 15 years later, a worker retiring in 1983 at the age of 65, earning the maximum of $7800 a year would still only get $188.80 and not the $218.00 per month.

The Dime Savings Bank of Brooklyn, New York, has recently widely publicized an advertisement labelled "How to Get Rich". This is what the chart showed.

"HOW MUCH WOULD YOU HAVE AT AGE 65?

EXAMPLES OF MONTHLY CASH PAYMENTS

Average yearly earnings after 1950 (1)	$899 or less	$1800	$3000	$4200	$5400	$6600	$7800
Retired worker—65 or older Disabled worker—under 65 }	55.00	88.40	115.00	140.40	165.00	189.90	218.00
Wife 65 or older	27.50	44.20	57.50	70.20	82.50	95.00	105.00
Retired worker at 62	44.00	70.80	92.00	112.40	132.00	152.00	174.40
Wife at 62, no child	20.70	33.20	43.20	52.70	61.90	71.30	78.80
Widow at 62 or older	55.00	73.00	94.90	115.90	136.20	156.70	179.90
Widow at 60, no child	47.70	63.30	82.30	100.50	118.10	135.90	156.00
Disabled widow at 50, no child	33.40	44.30	57.60	70.30	82.70	95.10	109.20
Wife under 65 and one child	27.50	44.20	87.40	140.40	165.00	190.00	214.00
Widow under 62 and one child	82.50	132.60	172.60	210.60	247.60	285.00	327.00
Widow under 62 and two children	82.50	132.60	202.40	280.80	354.40	395.60	434.40
One child of retired or disabled worker	-	44.20	57.50	70.20	82.50	95.00	109.00
One surviving child	55.00	66.30	86.30	105.30	123.80	142.50	163.50
Maximum family payment	82.50	132.60	202.40	280.80	354.40	395.60	434.40

(1) Generally, average earnings are figured over the period from 1950 until the worker reaches retirement age, becomes disabled, or dies. Up to five years of low earnings can be excluded. The maximum earnings creditable for social security are $3,600 for 1951–1954: $4,200 for 1955–1958; $4,800 for 1959–1965; and $6,600 for 1966–1967. The maximum creditable in 1968 is $7,800, but average earnings cannot reach this amount until later. Because of this, the benefits shown in the last two columns on the right generally will not be payable until later. When a person is entitled to more than one benefit, the amount actually payable is limited to the largest of the benefits.

IF YOU SAVE $50 A MONTH. . .

Your present age	At age 65, your account (including dividends) will be worth	Amount you will have actually deposited by age 65	Your Dividend Profit	If you leave the principal intact, dividends alone will give you this amount monthly for the rest of your life
25	$76,195	$24,000	218%	$317
30	56,771	21,000	170%	236
35	41,621	18,000	131%	173
40	29,803	15,000	99%	124
45	20,585	12,000	72%	85
50	13,395	9,000	49%	55
55	7,786	6,000	30%	32

So that at age 25, by making a monthly deposit of $50.00, an individual would have a nest egg of $76,195.00 when he reaches 65 with a monthly income of $317.00 for the rest of his life and his principal still intact. If at that time he wanted a larger income he could buy a single premium annuity with the principal and accumulated dividends from a most solvent insurance company which would guaranty him a monthly income of $570.04 for life, if male, and $498.77 if female. Since most people start earning their livelihood before 25 the savings and benefits would be increased substantially.

If the individual were otherwise financially well fixed, he could take his $76,000.00 and have one or more grand sprees or distribute it among his favorite charities or some poor relatives. No matter what his choice, by saving privately he would have contributed his capital to productive purposes thereby reducing the cost of living for the rest of us and would have done nothing to cause inflation which greatly reduced the purchasing power of government administered Social Security benefits.

Contrast this with the taxpayer's compulsory monthly contribution of $50.00 and more from employer and employee out of his pay envelope. From a dollar and cents standpoint Social Security makes no sense in providing so-called insurance or retirement protection. You get less for your money, and in addition you are contributing to the inflation which will and has caused you to get your pension paid in greatly depreciated currency. It is quite clear, that on a comparative basis, Social Security is a bad bargain, and if it were not compulsory it is doubtful whether it would be in operation at all.

In an article in *Barron's National Business Weekly* for April 26, 1965, commenting on the new Social Security bill just then passed by the House and awaiting Senate passage, there were set forth the following interesting figures and comparisons.

The new bill would require this worker and his employer to contribute an extra $4,240 for retirement. At the same time, the bill's 7% increase in cash benefits would mean an extra $1,667 for him. Thus, if HR 6675 becomes law, the 50-year-old worker can expect to make contributions of $26,012, including interest, against benefits of $25,592.

As for the 18-year-old, including the employer's contribution and figuring interest at 4¼% for the latter's 46-year working life (assumed by SSA) gives a total of $61,596, against $24,114 in benefits. For this contribution the worker could purchase from a private company a monthly annuity of $463 for life, after retirement. His maximum benefit under Social Security would be $254 a month.

Under the new bill, HR 6675, employer-employee retirement contributions for the 18-year-old, with 4¼% interest would come to $84,300. The 7% increase in cash benefits would bring the latter to only $25,802. For this amount, the worker could purchase from a private company a monthly annuity of $634 for life. His maximum benefit under Social Security would be $312 a month.

The bill was subsequently enacted into law.

Our government, in the nature of things, knows where the votes are and it therefore shows more interest in the voters of today than in the voteless youngsters who will have to pick up the tab in the years to come.

As we have seen, the idea of a Social Security System on a voluntary basis is a political hot potato and there is only the remotest chance whatsoever of its being permitted. On the contrary, it is quite certain that compulsory Social Security taxes and benefits will be expanded as they have been right from the start. The tax has increased about every other year during the past fifteen years or so. In 1937, the first year taxes were collected, nobody paid more than $30.00 in Social Security taxes. Thirty years later a worker would pay up to $290.40 and over the same period the combined tax including Medicare has gone up over $500.00. and now amounts to $580.80. President Johnson before his retirement promised that he would seek increased health benefits and enlarged Social Security payments in the years to come and President Nixon has already fulfilled his predecessor's promises.

Corresponding benefits for a worker at age 50 earning at least $7800 a year go from $155 monthly to $188.80 and for a married 50 year old worker from $231 to $305. For a 21 year old worker at present he would get maximum retirement benefits of $168 per month if single, which would increase to $252 if married. Under the current law a 21 year old single worker now being blessed with a Social Security member who retires at 65 would get $218 per month, as his maximum retirement benefit, again provided he always earned the maximum of $7800 per year creditable for Social Security. As we have seen, it would be a major miracle if the projected maximum retirement benefits for this young worker would equal in purchasing power the maximum retirement benefit now being received by the current pensioner.

In addition to the fact that retirement benefits under Social Security buy less now in purchasing power than they did when it started, there are other harmful side effects which should be mentioned. One such deleterious side effect would be the attempt of the employer to pass the Social Security tax on all along the line until the finished product reaches the ultimate consumer, thus causing pyramiding price increases.

One more injurious side effect of Social Security which is not too carefully evaluated is the inducement for workers to retire earlier than they normally would. In times of full employment or shortage of labor this will reduce the labor force and increase the cost of goods and services, thus further contributing to inflation. Does it make sense to persuade a low wage earner to retire at 65 and collect his Social Security pension which concededly is inadequate for him to live on and then have him apply for relief payments to supplement his Social Security? After all, he has paid in full for his pension, and since the Government persists in calling it "insurance" or an "annuity", in all fairness why shouldn't he get it, regardless of whether he continues working? In many countries, Italy for one, no penalty is attached in such cases but in America if a Social Security retiree earns more than $1680 a year ($32 a week), fully taxable incidentally both for income taxes and Social Security taxes, he loses all or part of his pension.

This feature of the Social Security Act has been widely

criticized and is obviously nonsensical when compared with the collateral section which for some mysterious reason permits anyone over 72 to continue working and still collect his Social Security in full, no matter what his earnings may be. I have never seen a rational justification of these utterly inconsistent provisions. The earnings penalty which restricts income for qualified Social Security recipients if they elect to continue working is a holdover from depression days and was intended to keep the old folks out of the labor market. It made no sense then and makes less today during an expanding economy and while inflation makes it impossible to get along on picayune Social Security benefits.

The psychological effect of too early retirement has been examined from time to time. It is not within the scope of this work to go too deeply into that subject other than to comment that very often this can prove quite harmful. There can be no arbitrary decision that retirement at 65 or at any other age is something desirable. We all know that in many cases the "twilight" years can be very productive depending on each individual's approach to life.

The Tax Foundation, a private non-profit organization founded in 1937 to engage in non-partisan research and public education on the fiscal and management aspects of government, issued a booklet in 1966 entitled "Economic Aspects of the Social Security Tax". It found that in 1966 the maximum Social Security Tax due from a given individual and his employer came to nine times the maximum when the system began.

The Tax Foundation commented that in spite of the increasing importance of the Social Security Tax as a revenue measure, (in fiscal 1967 it would account for about twenty percent of total collections) tax specialists and legislators knew very little about its economic effects.

The study noted that since the Social Security tax applies directly to wages and salaries, a firm's tax liability, generally speaking, will increase in approximate proportion to the number of employees or man hours it utilizes. Therefore, an employer might be inclined to try to reduce his liability for Social Security taxes by introducing or using more labor-saving machinery in order to reduce the man hours of labor required in his business. An example was given as to how this might work out in the hypothetical case of an average petroleum refinery. Suppose the corporation is considering the purchase of some new machine that will have a useful life of ten years and replace ten workers. After weighing successive and projected Social Security tax increases, the firm may find that the machine will produce enough Social Security tax savings to justify its purchase and the firing of the ten workers.

In the long run, automation has not reduced the work force. But in the short run it would have the effect observed in the example of the refinery, and those workers most likely to be displaced by the machine whose purchase became economically sound because of increased Social Security taxes, would be the least-skilled.

Another inequity which I have commented on earlier was also mentioned in the Tax Foundation study. The Social Security tax is imposed only on the lowest portion of an individual's earned income. In 1968 the base was made $7800.00. The result is that a worker with an annual income of up to $7800.00 pays an effective rate of 4.2% of his gross pay while his $20,000.00 a year boss pays 1.38% of his salary. This is a regressive tax. As the income gets higher and exceeds the base, the rate gets lower.

The Tax Foundation winds up its survey by observing that taxpayers have presented relatively little resistance to the tax. To date, it says, very few have opposed or criticized the Social Security tax and it wondered whether the apathy of the taxpayer would continue as the new schedule of higher rates goes into effect. I prophecy no opposition or resistance. The brainwashing has been successful, as evidenced by the fact that in 1969 alone 83,616,800 copies of 177 different publications and well over 100,000 newspaper releases, were distributed from Social Security headquarters and from the 800 Social Security offices in communities all over the nation. Each year Social Security makes wide use of magazines, radio and TV, motion pictures, displays and exhibits, lectures etc. We have been well conditioned. There will be no Boston Tea Party.

X

· · · · · · · · ·

The Rude Awakening

DURING the first few decades of the Social Security System there was very little critical public discussion of its deficiencies and inequities. One exhaustive analysis however was made by a prestigious critic as far back as 1950.

In the preface of a thorough study entitled "The Cost and Financing of Social Security" published by the Brookings Institution in 1950, the president of the Brookings Institution, H.G. Moulton, makes the following comment:

> The old-age and survivors insurance system in its present form involves constantly mounting costs over a fifty-year period. Great confusion has been engendered in the public mind because of the assumption that these costs can be gradually provided for through the application of ordinary insurance principles. That is, it is widely believed that the social security taxes now being paid furnish the resources from which the future benefits will be paid. The fact is that a practically universal governmental system cannot successfully apply the actuarial legal reserve devices of private voluntary insurance

systems. As the present system operates, no real reserve funds with which to meet future requirements are accumulated. The benefits will have to be paid out of future taxes.

Other critics have asserted that the trust fund is a fraud, since the government borrowings serve to create securities for the trust fund to acquire. One of these, Jo Bingham, in an analysis with the intriguing title "Social Security: Fair Words or Buttered Parsnips" (Twentieth Century Economic Thought, Philosophical Library Inc., 1950, p. 30) said "Summarily reviewed, debt is created by social security taxes in this manner."

Critics are becoming more outspoken and the Government increasingly is forced to acknowledge their criticism and is being put on the defensive. Witness this report of the Advisory Council on Social Security to the Senate Committee of Finance in which it attempts to justify the Government swindle of the trust funds.

This reserve has been invested in United States Government securities, which in the opinion of the Council represent the proper form of investment for these funds. We do not agree with those who criticize this form of investment on the grounds that the Government spends for general purposes the money received from the sale of securities to that fund. Actually such investment is as reasonable and proper as is the investment by life-insurance companies of their own reserve funds in Government securities. The fact that the Government uses the proceeds received from the sales of securities to pay the cost of the war and its other expenses is entirely legitimate. It no more implies mishandling of money received from the sale of United States securities to life-insurance companies, banks or individuals.

The investment of the old-age and survivors' insurance

funds in Government securities does not mean that people have been or will be taxed twice for the same benefits, as has been charged. The following example illustrates this point. Suppose some year in the future the outgo under the old-age and survivors' insurance system should exceed payroll tax receipts by $100,000,000. If there were then $5,000,000,000 of United States 2-percent bonds in the trust fund, they would produce interest amounting to $100,000,000 a year. This interest would of course have to be raised by taxation. But suppose that there were no bonds in the trust fund. In that event $100,000,000 to cover the deficit in the old-age and survivors' insurance system would have to be raised by taxation; and in addtion another $100,000,000 would have to be raised by taxation to pay the interest on $5,000,000,000 of Government bonds owned by someone else. The bonds would be in other hands because if the Government had not been able to borrow from the Old-age and Survivor's Insurance Trust Fund, it would have to borrow the same amount from other sources. In other words, the ownership of the $5,000.-000,000 in bonds by the old-age and survivor's insurance system would prevent the $100,000,000 from having to be raised twice—quite the opposite from the "double taxation" that has been charged. (U.S. Congress, Senate, The Reports of the Advisory Council on Social Security to the Senate Committee of Finance, Appendix I-A, "The Old-Age and Survivors' Insurance Trust Fund," Document No. 208, 80th Congress, 2nd sess. (Washington: Government Printing Office, 1949), p. 48.)

There can be no question but that the government must levy and collect taxes to pay interest on the obligations issued to the trust fund. Of course, these taxes do not pay Social Security benefits but are used for general government expenses for which the government took the money out of the Social Security "trust fund" in the first place and then used for foreign aid, defense, moon shots, etc. What the Government actually does is spend all the Social Security trust fund money, and then "invests" it in its own securities. Would the Government condone the "investment" by a life-insurance company of its reserves, if its directors "invested" the "reserves at a race-track, and then put an IOU in the till as evidence of the lost "investment"? Does it legitimatize the transaction if the insurance company then pays itself interest on the non-existent "reserves" represented by the IOU?

Let us contrast the Social Security pension set-up with that of a private insurance company. It should be noted in passing that in some other countries, Social Security funds may be invested in corporate securities. In any event if the government or an insurance company lent funds to a really productive private enterprise, it would then represent a true investment. The user of the capital so borrowed, would employ labor with this capital to enhance its productive capacity and permit it to pay true interest in an economic sense, to the lender of the funds.

In the government oriented plan embodied in Social Security, the Social Security taxes are spent by the Government, an I.O.U. is substituted and a book-keeping entry is made as a record of the taking. The money is never repaid, it is gone forever. To add insult to injury, the suckers who "contributed" the Social Security taxes in the first place, must now pay taxes to cover the interest on the IOU besides providing the cash to make good on the future Social Security payments as they become due. The speciousness of the government's defense by this time should be quite apparent.

The farce was thoroughly exposed in the study of the Brookings Institution referred to above. The authors wind up their keen analysis on this point at page 155 thus:

The establishment of the Trust Fund has given an aura of soundness and solvency to the OASI system. Many believe that this reserve fund "earns" income in the same sense as do private insurance reserves; that, if need be, all claims could be met by liquidation of the reserves; and that an individual, with his final payment of OASI taxes, will have paid in full for his retirement benefit.

The operation of the OASI Trust Fund is not similar in character to that of a private insurance company. Private insurance reserves, as noted above, are usually invested in projects that directly participate in or promote the production of goods and services. These investments are procreative in character and thus "earn" income. Furthermore, they are assets of the insurance company reserve, but they are liabilities of other enterprises. The OASI Trust Fund is invested in federal government securities. Since the money is used by the government in meeting its regular expenditure requirements, no real reserve is created. The obligations of the government (liabilities) deposited in a trust account do not represent assets; they merely record future obligations which can be fulfilled only through the levy of future taxes upon the economy in general. The Trust Fund is thus a fiction—serving to confuse.

Recently it is comforting to note a reaction to the euphoria seems to be taking place and criticism is becoming more widespread.

The October 1967 issue of the *Reader's Digest* carried an article entitled "How Secure is Your Social Security?" It created such a furor that about 500 elderly people picketed the New York offices of the magazine. *Reader's Digest* offices were also picketed in Philadelphia, Boston, Pittsburgh, Atlanta, Chicago, Detroit, Minneapolis, Los Angeles, and San Francisco.

The *Reader's Digest* article quoted Congressman Curtis, one of the country's most astute students of the subject as saying "If we don't do something fundamental to reform the System, I'm afraid it's going to hit the rocks in another ten years."

The storm aroused such disturbances that Wilbur J. Cohen himself, the architect of the Social Security System and thereafter appointed Secretary of the Department of Health, Education and Welfare, was caused to write a rebuttal which just did not rebut but mouthed the same old clichés and promised to make good on the Social Security promises. His rebuttal was placed in the Congressional Record of September 27, 1967, by Chairman Wilbur Mills of the House Committee on Ways and Means and is entitled "Statement by Wilbur J. Cohen about *Reader's Digest* Article 'How Secure is Your Social Security' ".

Mr. Cohen states categorically that the Social Security System is soundly financed; that future beneficiaries will be paid their benefits; that it is a sound and equitable program for the young and old. But the categorical statement is not proof and flies in the face of all of the evidence and facts and figures detailed in this book and in other works I have cited.

Robert J. Myers, while Chief Actuary of the Social Security Administration wrote a book which in a preface he declared was prepared outside of his official duties and responsibilities.(*Social Insurance Allied Government Programs* - Richard D. Irwin Inc.-1965) He discussed the question of the actuarial soundness of a pension plan and observed that some actuaries define an actuarially sound plan as one

Where the employer is well informed as to the future cost potential and arranges for meeting those costs through a trust or insured fund on a scientific, orderly program of funding under which, should the plan terminate at any time, the then pensioners would be secure in their pensions and the then active employees would find an equity in the fund assets reasonably commensurate with their accrued pensions for service from the plan's inception up to the date of termination of plan.

I submit that this definition is a fair one. Mr. Myers then concluded that according to this definition the Old-Age-Survivors, Disability Insurance System "is not actuarially sound".

In *The Roots of Capitalism* (Van Nostrand 1965) John Chamberlain wrote:

The answer of the Keynesians and the Veblenians to this emphasis on productivity will come wearisomely and insistently, and it it will take the form of the same old litany. "Capitalism," so they will say, "cannot be trusted to provide security without State intervention." The recent adoption of Medicare and the increase in social security payments are in line with this argument. But there are voluntary ways of doing all the things which the State is now doing at such a high inflationary cost.

Is it Social Security that the Keynesian is worried about? Well, why not permit any man who can prove that he is already paying his own insurance premium to be exempted from the Social Security Law? (The State might require for a transition period that he keep up a basic amount of private insurance at all times, but it makes no sense for Washington to insure Nelson Rockefeller.) Is it medical care beyond hospitalization that bothers our Veblenians? Well, the Blue Cross system, not to mention the private medical cooperative, is certainly capable of vast extension.—Is it the relief of the unemployed that seems an insurmountable obstacle under "laissez faire"? Well, why not grant tax rebates to any corporation which is willing to adapt the principle of the guaranteed annual wage to its operations?"

"Welfarism was private before it was public-and with productivity once delivered from the incubus of political inflation, the Welfare Society could easily outmatch and take over from the Welfare State.

Fortune Magazine for December 1967 carried as its lead article the subject "Social Security: Drifting off Course." It observed in pointing out its shortcomings, that the program, which began as an ad hoc response to the worst depression in the nation's history is now the focus of considerable, and growing concern. It noted that in current public discussion of Social Security, the almost reverent tone that formerly was used in commenting on this hallowed subject is being discarded in favor of a hard critical examination in the light of which the subject does not show up too well.

That analysis concluded as follows:

As a national ailment, poverty should be the responsibility of all society. The burden of financing old-age pensions for the poor, who cannot earn them through their own contributions, should be shared by all taxpayers, certainly not be borne by middle income families.

It is heartening to note many more critical magazine and newspaper articles, as well as radio and TV discussion programs, letters to the Editor, etc., all now raising serious doubts about the validity, soundness and integrity of Social Security.

Suggestions have been put forth by eminent economists such as Professors James M. Buchanan and Colin D. Campbell that the whole system be converted into one that is voluntary, less costly and actuarily sound.

In the *New York Daily News* of February 16, 1967, under the by-line of Dennis Duggan there was a full page devoted to the problems entitled: "Social Security: Where it Ends Nobody Knows". I quote some excerpts.

> Alarmed critics are wondering out loud if social security is leading us to national bankruptcy. Because each turn of the social security wheel that raises benefits and spreads coverage has to be greased with higher taxes on your earnings.—Today's program has as little in common with the original old-age survivor's program as a peacock has with a wart hog. . . .
>
> Who will pay for all this? Will rising income taxes and social security taxes prove too crushing a burden on the already burdened taxpayer?
>
> And finally, are today's younger wage-earners taking it on the chin to pay for the growing old age retirement, survivor's disability and health benefits available to the older workers?
>
> Those are some of the questions being raised as the social security program balls along a wide-open track. The answers aren't coming back loud and clear.

The following day another page was devoted to the subject under the heading "Social Security—Is It Welfare in Disguise?"

It began by stating three main criticisms being lodged against the ever-expanding social security program, as follows:

> 1) "What was once a straightforward old-age insurance program has been transformed into an outright welfare program.
> 2) The entire social security program is fiscally unsound.
> 3) A youth rebellion is brewing as a consequence of higher social security taxes to pay for increased benefits for already retired and disabled workers."

Also in the late N. Y. *World-Journal-Tribune* of February 1, 1967, in an article entitled "Costly Shenanigans of the Great Society", Henry J. Taylor wrote;

> *We Taxpaying Peasants* deserve to know why we've had 15 tax and/or wage base increases in 30 years, averaging one every other year, and although benefits have been increased 119 per cent the taxes we provide for these have increased 480 per cent.
>
> The whole business of Social Security, as now handled, cries out for a full and immediate investigation by the New Congress.
>
> Obviously, Johnson has a blind spot about money but it is impossible for me to believe his blind spot is as big as all this. He has had some experience in life and a 10 year-old boy should be able to see what is happening to the value of the dollar."

Unions too in recent years have been voicing increasing dissatisfaction. The United Auto Workers, which has its own Social Security Department, has gone on record in 1968 suggesting alternatives to what it calls the present unsatisfactory method of financing the Social Security System. It proposes three corrective measures for study and action as follows:

> (1) Provide out of general revenue of the United States Treasury enough money eventually to equal ⅓ of the cost of the program, observing that the United States is virtually alone in not making contributions to its Social Security program out of general funds.
>
> (2) Increase the covered earnings base to at least $15,000.
>
> (3) Exempt from payroll tax the first $600.00 of covered earnings.

The Union's first proposal bears the active endorsement of the late Senator Robert F. Kennedy and others in order to justify larger Social Security benefits.

The last two suggestions are designed to redress the increasingly regressive aspects of the present Social Security taxes.

Wilbur J. Cohen, former Secretary of Department of Health, Education and Welfare, acknowledges that there is now "moderate opposition coming from younger workers who are not happy about their Social Security taxes that the government says will take care of them in their old age".

Dr. Colin Campbell, a professor of economics at Dartmouth, who has made an extensive study of Social Security costs and benefits, finds that by private insurance company standards the younger workers are indeed right and are getting a bad deal. Every worker under 40 he contends would be much better off with a private insurance company and the younger the worker the better his private pension would be. In the article in *Fortune Magazine*, which I referred to above, his conclusions are stated as follows:

> To make his point, Campbell uses the example of a twenty-two-year-old who is entering the work force this year at a salary of $6,600. Assuming only presently scheduled increases in tax rates, the worker and his employer will accumulate a total of $68,000 during the forty-three years before he retires. (The figure includes $41,000 that the worker could have earned in interest on the money if it had not been held by the government.) If 20 percent of these contributions are assumed to have paid for the disability and life-insurance protection that goes with social security, then $54,000 was in effect used to purchase the worker's retirement pension. But if he and his wife live for the statistically average fourteen

years past retirement age, only $32,000, with the interest it
would earn, would be needed to pay benefits under current
schedules. Thus, Campbell asserts, the average young worker
at the upper end of the taxable income scale is being over-
charged by $22,000 for the benefits he will receive.

When we compute the cost of administering the government program, including the hordes of employees and all
related overt and covert expenses which must be absorbed by
the same worker when he pays his income and other taxes,
we can then judge how expensive and inefficient on an actuarial basis government "insurance" is as compared to true
private insurance.

Impartial evaluation therefore indicates that the benefits
that were to flow from the tax bite showering manna on all
of us, just never materialized.

The fact is that the Social Security tax tends to create
unemployment just as we shall see in Chapter XI minimum
wage laws do. Both are hailed by our "liberal" legislators as
harbingers of security but the inevitable result is more and
more social and economic insecurity.

Doing our arithmetic lesson shows us that a person just
starting to work in 1968 and earning at least $7800 - a year
for the next 43 years, will have paid Social Security taxes of
$66,442 for old age security alone by the time he retires at
65. When we realize, as we must, that the rate and the base
will surely increase during those 43 years, and we add a
similar sum taxed from his employer, the fraudulent nature
of Social Security becomes shockingly striking. If young
workers also did their homework, simple arithmetic would
reveal to them that the discounted value of their benefits
would never equal the taxes they pay plus interest and they
would have good reason to rebel against the iniquity so pi-

ously advanced for their ostensible benefit by their ever solic-
itous government.

It is encouraging to note the beginnings of awareness in
this regard in one of the economic resolutions adopted at a
recent congress of Young Americans for Freedom where
they came out for making participation in Social Security
optional. They were convinced by an analysis of the figures
along the lines I set forth above that an average worker could
earn as much higher income than his Social Security pittance
by investing this sum of over $66,000 deducted from his pay
in a most conservative fashion, even in a savings bank at 5%
interest and still leave the entire principal to his heirs. In
addition, of course, this same young worker pays the salaries
and incidental expenses of all those administering the Social
Security program for his so-called benefit, currently amounting to about a billion dollars annually.

The reaction of these aroused young Americans is reminiscent of the complaint of the colonists against King George III
as expressed in the dignified Biblical-sounding words in the
Declaration of Independence:

> He has erected a multitude of new Offices, and sent hither
> swarms of Officers to harass our People and eat out their
> substance.

At least King George was not a hypocrite and didn't tell
the colonists he was taxing them for their own good.

Increasing concern over the integrity of the Social Security
System has been sparked recently by the realization that no
funds have been set aside to cover $50 billion of the $68
billion of future retirements benefits earned by and scheduled
to be paid to 2.5 million Federal government employees as
of 1968. This deficiency is growing at the rate of $1.5 billion
annually.

The reassurance by the Government on that score is strangely reminiscent of its pledges as to Social Security. Deputy Budget Director Philip Hughes comments that with the "full faith and credit of the United States behind the system, the Federal Government's promise to pay retirement benefits to its employees is an ironclad obligation—The integrity of the System is not at issue".

However, scepticism creeps in and the credibility gap widens. Like the Social Security System, Federal Employees started to contribute 2.5% of their salary towards their pension "fund". It is now up to 6.5% established in 1957 with the Federal Government matching it and as of this writing a 7% rate has been projected. Again like Social Security taxes, this represents a substantial take out of the wage envelope on the promise of a future benefit which as to its future purchasing power is becoming increasingly difficult to measure with any degree of accuracy.

In concluding this Chapter, I should like to quote the observations of Mr. Justice Black of the United States Supreme Court in his dissenting opinion in the case of Flemming v. Nestor, 363 U.S. 603, referred to both in the *Reader's Digest* article and in Mr. Cohen's rebuttal placed in the *Congressional Record.*

The facts in that case were as follows:

Mr. Nestor came to America from Bulgaria in 1913 and lived here continuously for 43 years. In 1956 he was deported for having been a Communist from 1933 to 1939. During those years membership in the Communist Party was not a crime and was not even grounds for being deported. From 1936 to 1955 Nestor and his employers made their Social Security payments. In 1954, 15 years after Nestor had last been a Communist and 18 years after he and his employers made their Social Security payments, Congress passed a law that any person who had been deported because of past Communist membership should lose his Social Security benefits. After deporting Nestor in 1956, the Government notified his wife who remained in the United States that he would get no further payments.

The majority of the United States Supreme Court in a 6 to 3 decision upheld the Government. The majority opinion was written by Justice Harlan and while recognizing that the right to Social Security benefits "is in one sense 'earned' " he nevertheless wrote:

> That program [SS] was designed to function into the indefinite future, and its specific provisions rest on predictions as to expected economic conditions which must inevitably prove less than wholly accurate, and on judgments and preferences as to the proper allocation of the Nation's resources which evolving economic and social conditions will of necessity in some degree modify.
>
> To engraft upon the Social Security System a concept of "accrued property rights" would deprive it of the flexibility and boldness in adjustment to ever-changing conditions which it demands.

Mr. Justice Black wrote the dissenting opinion and in commenting on the majority opinion depriving Mr. Nestor of his Social Security benefits on the ground that he was once a Communist said the following:

> The Court consoles those whose insurance is taken away today, and others who may suffer the same fate in the future, by saying that a decision requiring the Social Security system to keep faith "would deprive it of the flexibility and boldness in adjustment to ever-changing conditions which it demands." People who pay premiums for insurance usually think they are paying for insurance, not for "flexibility and

boldness." I cannot believe that any private insurance company in America would be permitted to repudiate its matured contracts with its policyholders who have regularly paid all their premiums in reliance upon the good faith of the company.

Justice Black then made the further comment:

These are nice words but they cannot conceal the fact that they simply tell the contributors to this insurance fund that despite their own and their employers' payments to the Government, in paying the beneficiaries out of the fund, is merely giving them something for nothing and can stop doing so when it pleases.

So in essence what it boils down to is you pay your money and you take your chances. You are ordered to help pay a pension to a stranger and in order to lessen your obvious resentment you are assured that in the future some strangers will be compelled to pay you a pension too. The deal is always subject to change without notice and without your consent as the political climate of the times may dictate.

XI

• • • • • • • • •

The State—Friend or Foe

IN our search for security, the basic question of the role of the State must first be resolved. Is it the function of the State to look after the individual's welfare from the cradle to the grave? Should the State only worry about the individual for some lesser period—say from the age of sixty for women and sixty-five for men? Is it the function of the State to prevent the individual from the hazards of gambling, or from making a foolish business deal, or in general from making a jackass of himself? Does the government of the United States owe its citizens a guarantee of a job at a living wage or merely a guarantee of equal opportunity for each to earn his own living, as expressed in the concept of a fair field and no favor?

Albert Jay Nock in his classic *Our Enemy The State* made a clear distinction between Government and the State. The former he found to be an institution arising naturally with the growth of society and came into existence to serve its needs. He and other libertarians thought that the sole purpose of Government was to protect the individual from encroachment on the rights that are divinely and naturally his by virtue of his existence. Broadly speaking, the true business of Government is the exercise of its police power to preserve property rights, to preserve the peace and administer justice.

The State, however, did not arise out of necessity or any social need for it. It was and still is anti-social in nature, originating in conquest and maintained by force. It is concerned not with the production of wealth but with its appropriation or confiscation. In the old days, the State followed the precept of "To the victor, the spoils" by collecting tribute, appropriating the cattle and the women, and in general getting all the victors could for their trouble.

Unfortunately, today the distinction between the State and Government is rarely made and even more rarely understood. It should be recognized that there is a large segment of the American people whose faith in the State is profound and who would encourage and willingly support a greater role for it. Social Security is but one aspect of their undying confidence in the ability of the State to do more for the individual than he could possibly do for himself. Their adulation of the State is reflected in the aspirations and plans that were projected for the Great Society, and the Nixon Administration, some of which have already been initiated and some already aborted. To a great extent they believe that any social or economic problem can be solved by either passing a law, or by throwing money at it, or by a combination of those remedies, both at home and abroad. Social Security is a logical extension of this faith.

An example of this approach as a solution of our economic maladies is the minimum wage law. Wages are low at the margin of production. Therefore pass a minimum wage law to cover those low paid workers and thus increase their wages. What could be simpler? The State has thus shown its concern for the poor and if incidentally the Administration in power is rewarded with their votes, that is a by-product not entirely unexpected. Such legislation highlights the humanitarian feeling that low wages are undesirable and should be abolished, both in good times and bad.

The politicians are either ignorant of basic economic laws or deceitful or both. Wages do not depend on what Washington decrees they should be. If the poorly paid worker receives $1.25 an hour, passing a law compelling the raising of his wage to $1.50 or $5.00 an hour must be ineffective and disruptive. Temporarily a small number of workers may find their incomes increased. However wages can only come from production and not from an edict. Money is only a medium of exchange. If the worker produces $1.25 worth of X goods per hour and the State decrees he must be paid $1.50 per hour, one of two things happens. If his employer complies with the law and pays him $1.50 per hour for $1.25 worth of production, before long he will go bankrupt. The other, and more likely effect will be that the marginal worker will remain unemployed and a public charge as it no longer pays anyone to hire him.

Evidence has been adduced time and again that the general result of a minimum wage law is to increase unemployment among the least skilled workers. The political dishonesty or ignorance of the promulgators of minimum wage legislation is made clear when we think of how simple it could have been to pass minimum wage legislation during the big depression of 1929—1937. It was recognized then that such legislation would prove entirely futile besides being a cruel joke and a hoax.

In what is tantamount to an acknowledgment of its failure to solve the problem of the so-called "hard-core unemployment", the administration has dumped the problem in the lap of private industry.

The minimum wage laws are to a great extent primarily responsible for the fact that these marginal workers cannot get gainful employment in more or less prosperous times, as has been well documented by the research and study of Dr. Yale Brozen who is professor of business economics of the Graduate Business School of the University of Chicago. Dr. Brozen finds that before the minimum wage was increased in 1956, there was no difference in unemployment figures between white and non-whites. But after the effective date raising the hourly minimum wage in 1956 and since then the non-white group suffered greatly by comparison. Their rate of unemployment ranged between 50% to 150% higher than the white teenage males. As of October 1967 the unemployment rate was 10.7% for whites against 28.3% for non-whites.

Dr. Brozen concludes with this completely realistic observation:

> The greatest help we can give the Negro today, is to repeal the statutory minimum wage. By raising it, we are foreclosing opportunity for Negro teenagers who cannot get the jobs where they could learn the skills that would enable them to earn far more than the minimum.

Unemployment attributable to increases required by minimum wage laws falls most heavily on the very class that the legislators presume to help, to wit, Negro teenagers.

Everyone recognizes the misery caused by low wages but some professed cures only aggravate the illness. When the minimum wage was raised on February 1, 1967, to $1.40 an hour, non-white teen-age unemployment jumped in the very next month from 20.9 percent to 26.2 percent. The same pattern was evident the following year. When the 1968 minimum wage was again raised effective February 1, 1968, by the following month non-white teen-age unemployment soared from 19.1% to 26.2%.

A survey by the National Federation of Independent Business, Inc. having more than 250,000 member business proprietors indicates that as a result of the minimum wage law the annual rate of job loss by marginal and submarginal workers reached more than 680,000 in 1967.

Thus the whole idea behind minimum wage legislation misses the point. The problem is not low wages but low production. The absolute maximum wage a worker can receive presses against but can never exceed his production, and any minimum wage which exceeds his productivity must put him out of a job.

This digression about minimum wage laws merely points up how do-gooder tactics very often do evil things for those they are intended to help. To a great extent the same complaint can be levelled at hundreds of other political and pseudo-economic schemes, the effects of which are in many cases just as serious and far reaching as the Social Security System. Some of these, like minimum wage legislation, rent subsidies, and the Social Security System, up to now have been virtually immune from criticism for after all who would speak out against aid to the poor and downtrodden, and who would begrudge security and medical assistance to the aged and infirm? Is it not better and more noble to rest on the backs of the younger generation, than to depend on charitable and religious organizations, or public assistance, when misfortune strikes?

Another classic example of how the attempts of the public officials to repeal the law of supply and demand create havoc is reflected in the farm program designed to help the poor farmer. It is not within the scope of this work to point up the idiocies in that whole crazy quilt scheme of legislation. As so often happens from time to time, at the present writing there is a "revolt" of the housewives in an attempt to bring down the price of food that they are compelled to pay. But against whom are they revolting? They are not inveighing against the rise in Social Security taxes or minimum wage laws which must ultimately be reflected in higher prices but they are boycotting the retailers, and in particular the big chain stores. The State joins in the farce with a straight face to "protect" the consumer. An examination of the operating statements of these giants however shows that they earn less than 1c per dollar of sales. Obviously the blame for the high cost of food cannot be laid at their door since independent surveys have shown that the profit margins of big chains like A & P and Safeway are among the lowest of any industry and the retail food industry itself has been acknowledged to be fiercely competitive. Who then is responsible?

Are the farmers themselves then responsible? The big farmers, many of them operating in the corporate form, can do business profitably in a free market and are in no need whatsoever of price supports. It makes no sense to subsidize the tobacco growers and support the price of tobacco and at the same time urge people not to smoke. But a free market for farm produce will do away with a lot of jobs for the bureaucracy and very likely lose a lot of votes if by a miracle it should ever come to pass, since the farmers have gotten used to being treated as a specially favored group of citizens. Still the Department of Agriculture with the blessings of each new Administration continues as it has for the past few decades with its clumsy efforts to prop up the so-called small "family" farm which is rapidly disappearing. By its meddling with the free market mechanism, it has succeeded only in causing wasteful surpluses, high prices, and even dissatisfaction among those it purports to help.

According to a 1966 poll reported in the *Farm Journal*, 87% of 5000 farm owners and operators voted for cuts in Federal spending. They supported their spending views since 63% voted for getting the Government completely out of price support and control programs, even though they increase and put a floor under farm income. Another 27% voted for "some supports" and fewer controls. Only 10% thought the present farm program was satisfactory and should be continued along the same lines. But both the Johnson and Nixon Administration have continued to "help" the farmer whether he wants it or not. Papa knows best.

The food processors and distributors obviously can't be blamed unless they are unlawfully conspiring and operating as a monopoly in restraint of trade. The fact of the matter is that they too are competitive, otherwise they would have been prosecuted under the anti-trust laws.

Again it is the helping hand of Big Government that is the villain. American farmers are the most efficient in the world. Even Kruschev was full of admiration for them on his tour of the farm belt a few years ago. Instead of permitting the law of supply and demand to operate for certain farm produce, the helping hand of do-gooder Big Government substitutes subsidies and price supports in place of the market place. In exchange for votes and submission to controls, bureaucratic officials administering the Congressional farm program offer the farmer high support prices and subsidies at the expense of the consumer who doesn't have the intelligence to strike at the root of the problem. Our farm policy disregards the fact that the primary purpose of agriculture is not arbitrarily to raise incomes for the farmers alone as a favored class, but to produce food for the market place for ultimate consumption by all the people.

These three instances are but a small part of the Welfare State syndrome, some of whose other activities, like those mentioned in earlier chapters, are still further removed from the area of legitimate governmental action.

The fiction of building a Social Security reserve fund which has been set aside and invested to insure the ability to meet the claims as they mature has now outlived its usefulness. Perhaps it was necessary to employ that technique in the beginning to put it across. In any event it is now being suggested seriously that Social Security payments be made on a pay-as-you-go basis disregarding the deception of purporting to create a reserve fund for that purpose.

The truth is that Social Security has always been on a pay-as-you-go basis. When payments became due, there was no stored up fund out of which they were made, but such payments all came out of current tax collections as they do today. We have seen that the bonds in the "trust fund" are merely a record of how much money the government took in from Social Security collections and then borrowed from itself and spent for other purposes. I anticipate that some future administration will realize that a combined payroll tax for Social Security of much more than 11% in addition to all the other payroll deductions may be too hard to sell. It will prove to be much easier to keep liberalizing Social Security and Medicare benefits and make up the difference from the Treasury's general tax receipts and borrowings without relating the liberalized benefits to increased Social Security taxes which is the pretense currently in effect.

As pointed out in earlier chapters, inflation will continue in the future to reduce the value of all social security benefits. Despite the substantial tax increases paid by the producers of wealth since the inception of Social Security, the current payments received by the elderly retired buy less for them than when the program began. There is no reason to believe that this trend will be reversed.

The history of Social Security legislation follows the same pattern of the income tax in America. A direct tax on incomes when initiated in 1913, was found to be so opposed to the philosophy of our founding fathers, that it required the 16th amendment to the constitution to be passed before it could become effective. Like Social Security taxes, in the beginning it was relatively insignificant being only 1% over a single exemption of $3,000.00 with surtaxes starting at the $100,000 level. Only 37 people out of a thousand were affected, and no one contemplated that it could become what it has today. The foot gets in the door and the house and contents are then appropriated. Social Security tax rates too have increased more than 260 percent since 1949 and the projected increase will put it in the neighborhood of 453 percent by 1973 and so on and so on ad infinitum and ad nauseam.

What then is the answer to it all? How does the individual satisfy his craving for security in the United States today?

An astute answer was given 200 years ago by Adam Smith, and his pithy observation is even more pertinent now than it was then.

It is the highest impertinence of kings and ministers, to pretend to watch over the economy of private people and to restrain their expense. . . . They are themselves always, and without any exception, the greatest spend-thrifts in the society. Let them look well after their own expense, and they may safely trust, private people with theirs. If their own extravagance does not ruin the state, that of their subjects never will.

First and foremost then we must reduce the size of our government. The principle must be established that whatever the people can do for themselves should be withdrawn from the scope of governmental activity. The legitimate area of government should be confined to creating a fair field with no special favors or privileges for its citizens. The vast bureaucracy must be reduced and the most effective way to do so is to give it less money. Since the power of the State is in direct proportion to its income, let us reduce its income, and instead let those who earn the money dispose of it as they see fit.

The compulsory pension approach as embodied in the Social Security System holds out the illusion of security. In the process, as we have seen, as part and parcel of the Welfare State it destroys the initiative to produce and the savings of thrifty men which, in a relatively short period of time, made America the most powerful country on earth. Still security does not come with the receipt of Social Security checks— it remains an illusion. When we consider the tremendous strides made in our productive capacity by the cooperation of labor and capital in a relatively free society, it is inconceivable that all efforts seem to be directed to reverse the trend rather than encourage it.

Our own experience has also taught us that economic security does not come with the Welfare State and also that even if it did, security and happiness are not synonymous. After all, it is the relatively secure rich who patronize the psychiatrists hoping to overcome their basic feelings of insecurity and their other problems which their wealth failed to remedy. We recall Toynbee's analysis of challenge and response as the driving force that caused higher civilizations to evolve. If primitive man were secure in his cave and his animal wants supplied by others, we would probably still be in the stone age. It took insecurity and challenges to make him what he is today and we shall see whether state administered security will return him to his cave. We must not forget that Toynbee also pointed out that 19 out of 21 civilizations died from within and not by conquest from without.

If people were directly confronted with the problem and had to choose between security and freedom, perhaps they would opt for security. Unfortunately the proposition of making a deliberate choice is never presented that simply or in so stark a fashion. It was insecurity however that drove primitive man from his cave in the search for weapons for his protection and prompted him to make tools to enable him to increase his supply of food thus distinguishing him from the other animals. If he had been living in a Garden of Eden with all his material needs cared for he would never have developed into the genius or monster as we know him today but would still be an emasculated version of homo sapiens. There is no drive for self-improvement in security. Insecurity is inherent in life itself and acts as a powerful force in motivating human action to higher levels.

A gradual erosion of our liberties has taken place in the quest for security with the inevitable result that in the long run the individual finds he has abdicated more and more control over his own destiny. It may very well be as Keynes said that in the long run we will all be dead anyway but all during the long run and in the intervening short runs we are very much alive and suffer the consequences of the system under which we live.

De Tocqueville recognized this tendency of exchanging freedom for security long ago when he wrote:

"Americans are so enamoured of equality that they would rather be equal in slavery than unequal in freedom."

The only true security is an inner one. We must be left alone and be free to do as we like so long as each of us does not impinge on the reciprocal right of every other individual to do as he pleases. We need some insecurity and freedom to produce within our capacities and desires, and the freedom to decide how to dispose of what we produce, not to have it decided for us by the non-producers.

As for these non-producers who in their profound arrogance presume to be so omniscient, they should be put on the defensive. They should be made to realize that we are on to their con game, whether it is played for social security stakes or in some other form. All of their promises to give us security, to provide for our moral uplift and peace of mind should be treated with derision and contempt. If they themselves are not aware of it, we should let them know that at least we know they have nothing to give us, except what they have first taken from us. They should be made aware of the Bible story in which it was reported that it came to pass that the Israelites so resented the heavy yoke placed upon them that they stoned Hadoram, the chief tax collector to death. I am not recommending anything as drastic as that but merely suggesting that Bible stories can be very interesting.

So too, with the professional do-gooders. Society is made up of individuals and it is up to each of us to take care of himself as he sees fit, both materially and spiritually. If the individual operating under the rules of a free society makes a better man of himself morally, intellectually and economically, then the group and the nation must reap the benefits.

It has never been seriously suggested that the political ranks in America and elsewhere are filled with men of the highest calibre, ability and integrity. The facts seem to indicate quite the opposite. The administrators of the Great Society seem to be as full of the human frailties and moral weaknesses that beset us all. It would therefore seem fitting and proper to suggest to these frenzied politicians so bent on doing good for us and to us, "improve thyself first". Their enthusiasm is a poor substitute for intelligence. We should not forget H.L. Mencken's characterization of the State as "the common enemy of all well-disposed, industrious, and decent men."

Each new field in which the State decides to move, provides a justification for an increase in taxes, more bureaus, more jobs for the pompous officials who are put in charge, as well as the lesser deputies and mediocrities with whom they surround themselves. Social Security at the Federal level does not signify that the states and cities have abandoned the Welfare State at the local level. An example which comes to mind is the narcotics problem. The Federal Government has a narcotics bureau, New York State has one and New York City not to be outdone has one for itself too. There is rarely a pre-emption and hardly ever does any problem get solved so that the bureau charged with its solution can accomplish its purpose, go out of business and the job holders fired.

A pithy comment on this sad state of affairs is cited in "The New Deal in Old Rome" by H.J. Haskell. [Alfred A. Knopf 1947] He quotes the Governor of one of our states as follows:

> In these days we have to make promises that we know we can't carry out. We have to promise the old people pensions that would bankrupt the state if we paid them. We have to promise higher salaries to the school teachers, higher wages to the working people, higher prices to the farmers, bigger allotments of public funds from the federal government. I am ashamed of what I have done. But I wanted to win.

The history of freedom everywhere in the world is reflected in the application of the limitation of government power. The gradual and constant enlargement of the power of the State signifies the death of human liberty and the advent of tyranny. An alcoholic does not get cirrhosis of the liver overnight nor does a heavy smoker develop lung cancer suddenly. So it is with the erosion of our liberties and the gradual conversion to statism. The logical extension and perfection of the Welfare State will be the totalitarian state no matter what name may be euphemistically assigned to it while the inexorable process is going on.

The following extract from Buckle's *History of Civilization in England* (1857) while referring to France in the 19th Century should serve as a warning to us that those who do not learn from history are condemned to repeat it.

> In fact, the whole business of the state is conducted on the supposition that no man either knows his own interest, or is fit to take care of himself.
>
> In short, without multiplying instances with which most readers must be familiar, it is enough to say that in France, as in every country where the protective principle is active, the government has established a monopoly of the worst kind, a monopoly which comes home to the business and bosoms of men, follows them in their daily avocations, troubles them with its petty, meddling spirit, and, what is worse than all, diminishes their responsibility to themselves, thus depriving them of what is the only real education that most minds receive—the constant necessity of providing for future contingencies, and the habit of grappling with the difficulties of life.

This warning was repeated by Ortega y Gasset in his famous work *The Revolt of the Masses* (Norton 1931) in which he saw that the causes for the lamentable fate of ancient civilizations were at work in modern times. In the chapter entitled "The Greatest Danger, The State" he wrote:

> This is the gravest danger that to-day threatens civilization: State intervention; the absorption of all spontaneous social effort by the State, that is to say, of spontaneous historical action, which in the long run sustains, nourishes, and impels human destinies. When the mass suffers any ill-fortune or simply feels some strong appetite, its great temptation is that permanent, sure possibility of obtaining everything—without effort, struggle, doubt, or risk—merely by touching a button and setting the mighty machine in motion. . . . But the mass-man does in fact believe that he is the State, and he will tend more and more to set its machinery working on whatsoever pretext, to crush beneath it any creative minority which disturbs it—disturbs it in any order of things: in politics, in ideas, in industry.
>
> The result of this tendency will be fatal. Spontaneous social action will be broken up over and over again by State intervention; no new seed will be able to fructify. Society will have to live for the State, man for the government machine. And as, after all, it is only a machine whose existence and maintenance depend on the vital supports around it, the State, after sucking out the very marrow of society, will be left bloodless, a skeleton, dead with that rusty death of machinery, more gruesome than the death of a living organism.

In order to halt and reverse this lugubrious trend, the role of government should be limited to its police power of maintaining order, enforcing contractual obligations, and protecting property. The dignity of the individual as well as the common interest will best be served by each of us pursuing his own self interest in a competitive free-market economy.

Security and wealth will come or at least be available for those willing to work for it provided the government has provided the favorable climate and safeguards in the limited role thus prescribed for it.

Despite all its attempts to legislate poverty out of existence, the State in highly developed countries such as England, Germany, and the United States as well as an under-developed country like India, has uniformly failed to eliminate poverty. What the State has succeeded in doing perhaps is to eliminate starvation thru measures resembling the dole.

In the United States 6 out of 10 non-white children will have received public assistance thru the Aid to Dependent Families program by the time they become 18 years old. In the larger cities the problem becomes more acute with each passing year. As this is written more than 1,000,000 persons are on welfare in New York City. This is some 600,000 more than were on the relief rolls in 1941, which was the welfare peak of the big depression.

All the government palliatives have proven ineffective. When there are more jobs and opportunities in an expanding economy than there are prospective job-seekers, then only will poverty and slums be eliminated and true security prevail. And by jobs I don't mean in the armed services and in war industries or those performed by the more than 100, 000 full-time permanent employees in the Department of Health, Education and Welfare.

Social Security Systems of various shapes throughout the world clearly have failed to provide security. All they can do and have done is redistribute existing wealth without getting to the heart of the problem. In effect they retard and hinder economic progress thru their false promises and restrictive practices. The State has thus camouflaged the evil and by running wildly in all directions, and fighting "wars" on poverty conveys the impression that it is mightily concerned with the problem thus obscuring the true remedy.

This is not to suggest that in the event of a sudden catastrophe or during an emergency, that the government is to do nothing. What is proposed in the concluding chapter are some alternatives suggested to stop the growth of an all powerful state with the concurrent diminution of individual liberties.

XII

• • • • • • • • •

The Remedy

THE remedy guaranteed to cure the defects in our current Social Security System is its abolition. This may sound harsh and disdainful of the injunction contained in the United Nations Charter that "Everyone has the right to social security".

Since abolition of Social Security despite its inherent fraud, fiscal unsoundness, and all its harmful side-effects, is virtually impossible, it might be palatable if a suitable substitute can be found. Vested interests or special privileges are not freely abdicated.

One possibility does however present itself. I suggest that all who have paid into the Social Security System be re-paid in full with interest. It might also be feasible or practical in order to muster the necessary votes to insure the abolition of Social Security to add to the refund all the Social Security taxes that have been paid and credited to the workers' account by their employers. This total sum will then be paid to the employee covered by Social Security in the form of a "Federal Social Security Redemption Bond". The bond can be amortized at a fixed rate per annum say at 5% for those under 55 years of age, and at 10% for those over that age bracket, or amortization can be based on life-expectancy tables. The Social Security Redemption Bonds should be non-negotiable and payments would cease upon the death of the holder and the bond cancelled at that time. Payments should come out of general tax revenues.

This is a broad and sketchy outline of one way of redressing a wrong and making an innocently defrauded person whole.

There are some eighty million taxpayers who simultaneously with their "Social Security Redemption Bonds" would also immediately get a substantial increase in pay as a result of its repeal. In addition, production would be stimulated, prices would fall and inflation would be slowed and perhaps reversed thereby enhancing the purchasing power contained in the workers' pay envelopes considerably.

If this seems too drastic and politically inexpedient considering the fact that there are now 25 million persons on Social Security in America, who together with their relatives represent in the neighborhood of 80 million votes, there are other alternatives. It might be replaced by a dignified system guaranteeing to those in need no matter of what age a decent minimum standard of living depending on the state of the economy at the time in question if they are unable through no fault of their own to provide for themselves. America is wealthy enough to insure that no one need be ill-fed, ill-housed, or ill-clothed if he is unable to provide for basic needs himself. And that goes for medical care as well. Certain safeguards must be set up, such as a means test, degrees of consanguinity to be held primarily responsible, etc. Current general tax revenues would be used as they now are, to make the payments. There will be no fictitious reserves, no ephemeral "trust funds", no elaborate fiction of operating a truly funded insurance annuity program, and no jockeying for votes at every election time when each party vies with the others in promising greater benefits. Congress will not have to be engaged in the fortune telling business by attempting to predict what tax and revenue rates will be required twenty years hence to provide dollar amounts for unpredictable needs at an unforseeable price level for future generations.

We must also remember that not everyone over 65 is destitute. In 1966 the total income of the elderly over 65 was $40 billion. About ⅓ of them had assets—not including the value of their homes, of $10,000 or more (*New York Times* 2/5/67). A goodly portion of these of course had purchased annuities from private insurance companies, or had company pensions, and in addition union pensions. Sprinkled among the beneficiaries of Social Security are some millionaires also.

Nor should it be thought that Americans gave no thought to insuring themselves against the hazards and expense of illness before the advent of the Government Medicare plan. Enrollment had reached the highest point in Blue Cross history by the end of 1967. In the United States Blue Cross provided hospital protection for one out of three Americans, over 62 million being enrolled by the end of 1967 as compared to 50 million 10 years earlier. In 1966, Blue Cross entered into a contract with the United States government to administer Medicare for it for persons over 65.

The Internal Revenue Service reports that for the first 9 months in 1966 there has been a tremendous growth in the number of qualified pension plans. *Business Week Magazine* also reported that in the same period more profit sharing plans were initiated than in all of 1965 and that plan assets have shot up from $5 million in 1946 to $18 billion in 1965 in which year $1.2 billion was paid out to participants and that over 5 million workers were covered. Most of the larger companies have both profit-sharing and pension plans. Such private pension plans not only provide income after the employee retires, but can also be a source of money for the beneficiary of the employee who dies prior to retirement. The death benefit of an insured pension plan is automatic and is usually $1000 for every $10.00 of monthly retirement benefit. This trend is increasing and this is the kind of alternative to Social Security that should be encouraged by the Federal Government through tax concessions.

When to this substantial number of workers who have thus arranged their own security there is added the number who would or could have provided for their retirement if there were no Social Security taxes, it is quite evident that in a prosperous America there would be no great need for a compulsory Social Security System.

There are some people who are opposed to Social Security taxes on religious grounds and have refused to accept Social Security payments as a matter of principle. The Old Order Amish people are an example of this. An Amish bishop quoted in the *U.S. News and World Report* (7/24/61) said:

> We feel it is the duty of the father to help his children get on their own farms. Then, when we get older, we look for the children to return again and take care of us as we need it. So far as Social Security is concerned, we just don't need that. We do not want it. We do not intend to accept it.

Anyone who has seen the Amish farms around Lancaster and York, Pennsylvania, and in the Mid-West will appreciate that these hard working, religious people will never become relief cases.

However Uncle Sam decreed no exceptions, and went so far as to attach three work-horses from an Amish farmer and sell them at public auction to cover the Social Security taxes he owed (*New York Times* 5/2/61).

There is no reason why a taxpayer should not be permitted a choice of providing for his own security in lieu of being forced to take the government sponsored plan. We have seen in Chapter VIII, that for the same amount of money the worker can get a far better deal by merely putting an equivalent sum in a savings bank regularly. The salutary side effects that this type of saving would have on the economy are self-evident when contrasted with the deleterious effects of the government Social Security System. At the same time in the event of individual misfortune, a wealthy country like ours can well afford to be generous, to say nothing of private charities coming to the rescue on a more personal level.

The answer is quite clear that the government does not want any competition. It has pre-empted the field because it cannot stand the challenge of submitting to a standard of comparison.

In the interview reported in Chapter III with Robert M. Ball, Commissioner of Social Security, he was queried about this very point.

Q. — From the standpoint of the typical worker, is Social Security a good buy? Would it be correct to say that no worker could buy private insurance to provide what Social Security does at a cheaper price than the tax he pays? A. — Yes, I would say that. And it's primarily because of the employers' contributions.

The thought immediately comes to mind that if Social Security is such a great bargain, why the fear of permitting a voluntary program so that a worker can opt out of the Government one?

In *Time* magazine (10/23/64) an anonymous expert gave his opinion that if Social Security were put on a voluntary basis, and if only 15% of 1964's workers under 30 paying Social Security taxes elected to withdraw, the 1965 loss in Social Security taxes would be $1½ billion; by 1968, 8½ billion, and by 1988 the Social Security System would be bankrupt.

We have already seen that there is virtually no cash in the so-called Social Security trust or reserve fund. It is full of I.O.U's with no collateral other than the taxing power to back them up. It is hard to conceive of a more hopelessly bankrupt organization than the Social Security System anyway so why this great fear of bankruptcy foisted upon the unsuspecting American public? If the elderly had to depend on the money in the "trust fund" for their monthly checks, it would be pathetic as there would be no checks in the mail next month.

It is not within the scope of this work to outline in great detail all possible substitutes for the current Social Security System. It is hoped that sufficient evidence has been adduced to establish that a hoax has been perpetrated upon the American people.

It has been suggested that perhaps another alternative would be some sort of guaranteed annual minimum wage which seems as of this writing to be the next target at which labor unions are aiming and a "guaranteed annual income" being promoted by President Nixon. The basic difficulty with the several proposals for a guaranteed annual wage and guaranteed annual income aside from the economic fallacies pointed out in the previous chapter and the disincentive to work is that in order to be effective, such guarantees must of necessity be coupled with assurances to business of a guaranteed annual profit. When we get to that point, the pretense of working within a capitalist economy should be abandoned and socialism or communism embraced wholeheartedly. It is hoped that labor unions and the Nixon administration will realize this before it is too late. Capitalists should retain the freedom to go broke also.

Prof. Milton Friedman of the University of Chicago is a highly respected economist and a staunch individualist. In his book *Capitalism and Freedom* (Univ. of Chicago 1962) he first seriously proposed the idea of a negative income tax. He points out that in effect we now have a government guarantee of a minimum annual income although circuitously arrived at. Under his proposal, the individual or family unit would receive a direct subsidy from the Federal Government upon the filing of income tax returns showing inadequate income to insure a decent minimum standard of living, and no other independent resources to make up the deficiency. This would be a substitute for and not an addition to the hodge-podge welfare payments now being made.

Prof. Friedman acknowledges the dangers inherent in his scheme when he says in his book:

> The major disadvantage of the proposed negative income tax is its political implications. It establishes a system under which taxes are imposed on some to pay subsidies to others. And presumably, these others have a vote. There is always the danger that instead of being an arrangement under which the great majority tax themselves willingly to help an unfortunate minority, it will be converted into one under which a majority imposes taxes for its own benefit on an unwilling minority.

All of these suggested remedies miss the point. If an individual has a sufficient income, no matter from what source derived, that provides him with a decent livelihood, there is no reason why he should have to be dependent on or get a handout from his government. If the government doesn't take too much out of the worker's pay envelope and stops inflating the economy and permits the unhampered operation of capitalism, he will have the wherewithal to accumulate personal savings voluntarily, purchase his own annuity if he is so inclined, or otherwise look after himself. If he chooses to become a bum, then let him exercise his freedom in that respect also, but not at public expense.

The yearning for security can only be satisfied if the individual is permitted to freely develop his own skill and exert his own efforts as he alone sees fit. This must be accompanied by the freedom to use his entire production for himself, save it as capital to enable him to produce more efficiently or to freely exchange it, destroy it or give it away. This right to be secure in his property is burdened with the responsibility to recognize and protect the same rights in others and is subject to taxation for legitimate governmental purposes.

Americans enjoy the world's highest standard of living, despite many restrictive laws limiting production. We do not get wealthier by producing less and the reason this country is rich is that up to now there were relatively fewer restrictions on the producer's right to the fruits of his labor than in other lands.

True security rests in the preservation of individual liberty and private property. The slow and steady erosion of security in America can be measured by the corresponding increase of State power. It would be logical to infer that security would be enhanced in the machine and computer age but we find the reverse to be true. We produce more and become more insecure at the same time.

Security will never come from a Social Security System in an expansive Welfare State. It can only be realized when the source of security is discovered to lie within the individual himself. This simple truth makes it mandatory that the collectivist trend acquiring such great momentum in the 20th century must be reversed. It may be too late because power is not freely abdicated. The remedy requires that the people must reacquire the liberties they gradually surrendered to the State.

The State has increasingly intruded by meddling legislation into areas which it should scrupulously avoid and which are and should be reserved for private action, for better or for worse. The most effective way of reducing its power to interfere with our liberties is to keep it broke.

Prestigious economists with an assist from the politicians are almost unanimous in urging that income taxes be raised to curb inflation and that Social Security taxes be raised and used as a tool to help accomplish the same result. I am not a professional economist but do have a smattering of knowledge in that field. Inflation has been defined, correctly, I think, as too many dollars chasing too few things.

Now, taking these dollars from my pocket and putting them in yours does not reduce their quantity in circulation or increase production. I have never been able to understand why a surtax added on to all other taxes is needed to curb the appetites of the producers of wealth to insure that they produce or consume less while at the same time it is perfectly proper for the Central Government to take that same wealth and continue to dispose of it, as in its supreme wisdom, it sees fit. All that higher Social Security and income taxes would accomplish would be to give the already gorged state more dollars to squander and further enhance its power, already swollen far beyond reason. The State has created the very condition it now laments and belatedly seeks to correct. It alone controls the supply of the number of dollars, pounds, marks, etc., it chooses to put in circulation to facilitate its borrowing and spending without producing. Ergo the transfer of my money to its coffers seems to make no sense as a cure for inflation. It points up the theory being advanced at all government levels with increasing speed as "You earn it, I'll spend it wisely". It seems to me that the only way to stop and reverse this trend is to starve the State by reducing its income.

President Johnson once laid it on the line quite bluntly in a speech he made on January 15, 1964, when he said:

> We are going to try to take all of the money that we think is unnecessarily being spent and take it from the 'haves' and give it to the 'have nots' that need it so much.

The income tax and the Social Security System and the negative income tax are the tools his successors will use to make his boast come true and it will come into being under the name of liberalism designed to give America's economically underprivileged "a better shake" and thus avoid violence threatened by the militant poor in our urban centers.

Liberalism today seems to be synonymous with this aggrandizement of the Welfare State. I submit real liberalism is really just the opposite, being more accurately defined by Herbert Spencer when he wrote in 1892:

> The function of Liberalism in the past was that of putting a limit to the powers of kings. The function of true Liberalism in the future will be that of putting a limit to the powers of Parliaments.

There are two evident truths which I trust have come into sharp focus in this book. Firstly, as highlighted in the analysis of the Social Security System, is the simple fact that the State has nothing and therefore cannot give anything to its people that it first doesn't take from them. All its myriad social services including Social Security, price supports and subsidies, etc. are purely and simply schemes for redistributing wealth.

The second simple truth is referable to the destruction of values resulting from the Government's acts involved in this giant effort to attain security via the political means. It is that all inflation is government made.

With all the discussions and hoop-la about cradle to the grave security administered by a concerned and magnanimous State, we might with profit review what the eminent historian and scholar Edward Gibbon wrote many years ago about the ancient Athenians in his famous work on the decline and fall of the Roman Empire. From being the center of the civilized world for over 500 years, Athens collapsed, never again to rise to its former high estate. In analyzing the reasons for its decline and fall, Gibbon wrote:

> In the end, more than they wanted freedom, they wanted security. They wanted a comfortable life and they lost it all —security, comfort and freedom. When the Athenians finally wanted not to give to society, but for society to give to them, when the freedom they wished for most was freedom from responsibility, then Athens ceased to be free and never was free again.

It happened both in Athens and Rome, as well as in other city-States and nations. The cause for the decay was internal and not due to external forces, all part and parcel of the quest for security.

Since I have made it quite clear that the Social Security System will not be abolished and since there is virtually no likelihood of the State's power being diminished and certainly no chance of the State voluntarily abdicating its power, why bother writing this book? Social Security is not the only fraud and deception being perpetrated and after all some people do benefit so why get so exercized about Social Security?

I confidently predict the decline and fall of our civilization. This lugubrious prophecy is based upon an historical analysis of the collapse and disappearance of other so-called advanced civilizations in the past which contained the seeds of destruction within themselves. The same conditions are present which were responsible for their demise and there is no reason to doubt that the same causes will not bring the same effects.

Nevertheless there was a compulsion to write about the current situation as an intellectual diversion and the Social Security fraud was the vehicle which prompted it. Theoretically there is still hope that a miracle might occur. There are some who have pondered the question as to where we are drifting and whether there is anything that can be done to stop going along with the tide. It is to that remnant that I dedicate this book and suggest a slogan which they might adopt as a course of action for themselves and an example for others.

Ask not what your government can do for you; ask not what you can do for your government; ask what you can do for yourself—and do it.

Afterword

• • • •

Though 25 years have passed since the publication of *The Social Security Fraud*, the same pay-as-you-go system remains in place. Despite my warnings and those of my predecessors, many Americans remain confused about, or simply deny, the precariousness of the current Social Security system.

Politicians claimed to have "saved" the system in the early 1980s, but they merely forestalled disaster. The usual suggested panaceas—tinkering with payouts, increasing the retirement age, raising taxes, and assessing means tests—will not cure a conceptually flawed system. Even the generous estimates of Social Security's own statisticians indicate that by 2030 the Old-Age and Survivors Insurance and Disability (OASDI) Trust Funds will be bankrupt.[1] To cover benefits beyond 2015, taxes will have to rise to 17 percent of gross income.[2]

To make matters worse, within 35 years there will be fewer than two workers paying taxes for each retiree receiving benefits—a truly disturbing fact considering that in 1950 there were 20 wage earners for every beneficiary. How workers, 76 percent of whom pay more Social Security taxes than federal income taxes, can continue to support the aging population is unknown.

Intelligent action is needed while there is still time. Disaster can be averted if we return to individuals the responsibility for planning for their Golden Years. In 1971 I wrote: "The remedy

---

1. William J. Shipman, "Retiring with Dignity: Social Security vs. Private Markets," The Cato Project on Social Security Privatization, August 14, 1995.
2. Mark Skousen, "$4,000 A Month From Social Security?", *The Freeman*, June 1995.

guaranteed to cure the defects of our current Social Security System is its abolition." This still holds true today. But as I said then, such action would only be palatable to the armies of politically powerful seniors if a suitable substitute could be found.

That "suitable substitute" I hoped for in 1971 could be a variant of Chile's present social security system. Until May 1981, Chile operated a flawed pay-as-you-go system much like our present Social Security system. In the late 1970s Chile was faced with a dilemma. Benefits exceeded taxes, and the system had no reserves. José Piñera, who was minister of labor at the time and who is responsible for the major overhaul of social security in Chile, described the old system as having "a fundamental flaw, one rooted in a false conception of how human beings behave. That flaw was lack of a link between what people put into their pension program and what they take out."[3] The subsequent experiment with privatization and abandonment of all-out wealth transfer has been successful and popular among the Chileans.

Chile's new system is based on individual capitalization. Workers must contribute 10 percent of their wages to a private AFP (Administradoras de Fondos de Pensiones), which is similar to a mutual fund. AFPs invest the contributions in stocks, bonds, and government debt. When a worker reaches retirement age, he transfers the funds of his AFP account into an annuity with an insurance company or chooses a phased withdrawal. In the end, the average retiree receives a benefit that is almost 80 percent of his average annual income over the last 10 years of his working life.[4]

Chilean workers also have an advantage that American par-

3. José Piñera, "The Success of Chile's Privatized Social Security," *Cato Policy Report,* July/August 1995, p. 1

4. Shipman, *op. cit.,* p. 7.

ticipants in the Social Security system do not enjoy—the expertise of Wall Street managers and analysts. The two largest AFPs are owned and operated by U.S. investment firms (Bankers Trust and Aetna). Astute Chilean workers quickly took advantage of their new-found freedom. Over 1,400,000 immediately changed to the AFP system from the state system.

Currently, 93 percent of the Chilean labor force is enrolled in 20 separate AFPs. Competition keeps the AFPs on the lookout for good, sound investment opportunities. If a worker is not happy with his AFP, he is free to choose another one, as do some 500,000 workers annually.

The greatest difficulty faced by the Chilean government as it began plans to privatize the system was in deciding what to do with those who had originally contributed into the old state system. This problem must also be faced when we replace our system. Like Chile we must meet the dilemma with practicality. Chile accepted that she made a Faustian bargain with her workers in 1924 when she became the first nation in the Western Hemisphere to initiate a government-run social security program. Chile solved the dilemma by offering two alternatives to the workers who had paid into the state system: (1) remaining in the system, or (2) moving to the new system and accepting "recognition bonds" that acknowledged their contributions to the old system and were redeemable upon retirement. New workers, of course, must go into the AFP system. And when the last person who contributed into the old state system dies, the Chilean government will be completely out of the pension business.

This switch to the AFP-oriented system has been a boon to the country. Domestic savings—the bedrock of capital formation and thus economic growth—has skyrocketed to 26 percent of GDP. AFPs have purchased over 50 percent of the bonds issued by Chilean businesses, and with an annual growth rate that has averaged 5.4 percent from 1984 to 1992, Chile is the envy of the Southern Hemisphere.[5]

Though the United States has not yet learned from the Chilean example, several other nations have. Even Mexico, whose social security system is described as the equivalent of our system plus "Medicare, Medicaid, the National Endowment for the Arts and even Club Med and Wal-Mart," plans to turn some pensions over to the private sector.[6] Argentina, Peru, Colombia, and Italy have all privatized portions of their social security systems along the Chilean model. Certainly the model is not perfect, but it is the first serious attempt at abandoning the failed pay-as-you-go systems that do not adequately provide for retirement even as they cruelly plunder the younger generation. "The Chilean experience shows," says Social Security expert Peter Ferrara, that "it is possible to fulfill the obligations made to retirees in a government-run system while still letting workers move into a new, privatized one—all without suffocatingly high taxes."[7]

Our government should heed the Chilean example, but not follow it blindly. Any privatization plan here should avoid the traps that the Chilean government fell into. For instance, the Chilean requirement that AFP portfolios have at least 50 percent of their assets in government securities should not be imitated. Even though the 50 percent requirement would be an improvement over the current practice of investing all "surplus" OASDI receipts in U.S. Treasury securities, we can do much better. Such practices disguise the actual size of the federal budget deficit and fool the people into thinking that things aren't really so bad.

5. Skousen, *op. cit.,* p. 396.

6. Anthony DePalma, "Insecurity Rocks Mexico's Cradle-to-Coffen System," *The New York Times,* November 13, 1995, p. A4.

7. Peter J. Ferrara, "The Social Security Mess: A Way Out," *Reader's Digest,* December 1995, p. 109.

Furthermore, in Chile the government still guarantees a minimum pension. The fundamental idea that it is not the government's province to act as a charity has not been forsaken. When the government transfers wealth, it engages in, to use Frederic Bastiat's expression, legalized plunder—the basis of the modern welfare state.

Countless individuals have suffered from Social Security's plunder and have been cheated out of a dignified retirement. Had we privatized our system earlier, an individual born in 1970 and permitted to invest in stocks what he presently pays in Social Security taxes could expect nearly 6 times the benefits he is currently scheduled to receive upon retirement from Social Security.[8]

Fortunately, the intellectual environment has changed since the publication of *The Social Security Fraud* in 1971. Over the past 25 years the friends of freedom have had great influence. Even *Time* magazine ran a cover story on March 20, 1995, entitled "The Case for Killing Social Security." The article just stopped short of endorsing the Chilean model. *Business Week* (March 27, 1995), *The Freeman* (June 1995), *Reader's Digest* (December 1995), and several other national publications have also recently run articles that praised the Chilean reforms and prospects for reform in the United States. In 1971 such diverse voices clamoring for major Social Security reforms went unheard.

Nevertheless, we still have a long way to go in educating the public and politicians. Social Security is still off the table in spite of the so-called "Republican Revolution." Polls show that more young Americans believe in UFOs than believe they will receive Social Security benefits, and rightly so. The current Ponzi scheme cannot last long into the next century. The pol-

8. Shipman, *op. cit.,* p. 1.

iticians must level with the people about the choices ahead before disaster hits. As did Chile, we must abandon the ways of the past and follow the path of freedom into the future.

New York, New York, January 1996

Index

• • • •

About the Publisher

• • • •

The Foundation for Economic Education, Inc., was established in 1946 by Leonard E. Read to study and advance the moral and intellectual rationale for a free society.

The Foundation publishes *The Freeman*, an award-winning monthly journal of ideas in the fields of economics, history, and moral philosophy. FEE also publishes books, conducts seminars, and sponsors a network of discussion clubs to improve understanding of the principles of a free and prosperous society.

FEE is a non-political, non-profit 501 (c)(3) tax-exempt organization, supported solely by private contributions and the sales of its literature.

For further information, please contact The Foundation for Economic Education, 30 South Broadway, Irvington-on-Hudson, New York 10533; telephone (914) 591–7230; fax (914) 591–8910; e-mail freeman@westnet.com.